# OUTSTANDING PRAISE FOR *EMERGENCY!*

"If you are one of the millions of Americans who can't imagine a Thursday night without TV's *ER*, this book will bring you even more drama from the hospital."

—*Denver Post*

"The stories in *Emergency!* make the hit TV show *ER* look like Marcus Welby."

—*Colorado Springs Gazette Telegraph*

"Brown's stories are heartbreaking on one page, and breaking you up on the next ... You won't be able to read just one."

—*Abilene Reporter-News*

"True and deeply moving."

—*Wisconsin State Journal*

"If you're a fan of the TV series *ER*, you'll get a real shot in the arm from *Emergency!*"

—*San Antonio Express News*

"A compilation of 'you won't believe it' stories ... some are funny enough to produce belly laughs ... others provide a somber look at 'the anguish, fear, need and gore' doctors and nurses routinely face."

—*Rocky Mountain News*

"Physician Mark Brown strikes just the right note in this bestselling collection—neither maudlin nor cavalier but equally respectful of patients and doctors who treat them."

—*The Cleveland Plain Dealer*

"Tense, poignant, and amusing."

—*Publishers Weekly*

# EMERGENCY!

## TRUE STORIES FROM THE NATION'S ERs

COMPILED BY

## MARK BROWN, M.D.

St. Martin's Paperbacks

Published by arrangement with Villard Books.

EMERGENCY!: TRUE STORIES FROM THE NATION'S ERS

Copyright © 1996 by Mark Brown

Cover photograph by Ron Chapple/FPG International.

ISBN: 0–312–96265–7

Printed in the United States of America

Villard Books hardcover edition/January 1996
St. Martin's Paperbacks edition/September 1997

St. Martin's Paperbacks are published by St. Martin's Press, 175 Fifth Avenue, New York, NY 10010.

10   9   8   7

# CONTENTS

# CONTENTS

**CONTENTS**

# INTRODUCTION:
# THE DOORS

Emergency rooms have no windows. They have doors. The pneumatic type, that open unexpectedly with a hiss. Inside the doors is a family of specially trained people who work, prepare, and wait. They wait to see what the doors will bring. Pain, fear, anguish, irritation, and embarrassment are some of the visitors. They come at any time, with any intensity, in any number. There is no order to their arrival. Those entering all have one thing in common—they need help from the people inside.

The business of the world outside is unseen until a soft hiss announces the arrival of the world's business gone bad. The doors bring cute kids with splinters right after cute kids covered with blood from gunshot wounds. Basketball players with swollen ankles precede grandmas gasping for breath. Poor people with colds enter with SIDS babies and screaming drunks.

The disorder of arrivals creates tensions inside as the workers are buffeted by suddenly changing needs. Maintaining a high level of readiness is tiring, and efforts of the specialists may appear wasted on scraped fingers and colds. The very ill bring their own emotional charge, which must be matched in order to maintain control. The patient must never smell fear. Nights bring their own punishment: The self is screaming for sleep; the patient is screaming for help. What at four in the afternoon seems challenging, at four in the morning is grueling.

The doors also take people out. Sometimes the people are relieved and comforted. Sometimes they are angry. Sometimes they leave with unknowable grief. Sometimes they leave dead.

The emergency room is a cauldron of human emotions. The anguish, fear, need, and gore is wearing. As the protective layer of the self is weakened, the pain seeps through and begins to stain the soul. The protective layer grows thicker. But the patients' needs call out to a sensitive heart, and a balance is struck. Survival in this place requires a deep kindness nestled in a very dark sense of humor, and a strong faith tempered with cynicism. The people who work in this place refer to it as the Pit.

What follows is a collection of true stories from all over the country about what the ER doors bring. These stories are irreverent, funny, horrifying, and heartbreaking. They will buffet you.

These stories are presented randomly, not neatly categorized as one might desire but in the disorderly manner in which the doors might bring them. They are written not by writers and reporters but in the words of the doctors, nurses, and paramedics who were there.

I hope these true stories give you an appreciation of what goes on behind the doors.

MARK BROWN, M.D.
*Malibu, California*

# PROLOGUE: ON BECOMING A DOCTOR

I might never have become a doctor but for a visit I made to my brother more than twenty-five years ago. He was a medical intern in Madison, Wisconsin, and I, well, I wasn't much of anything. I was getting ready to quit my job with *The New York Times*, and had no idea what to do with the rest of my life. I really wanted to be a writer, but in some fundamental way I knew I wasn't yet ready to write: I hadn't lived enough, or experienced enough, to have anything important to say.

As the intern in the ER (all of about one month out of medical school), Robert was the only doctor in the department. He could, of course, call for help (but only if he were willing to admit he was such a wimp as to need any). His supervising resident (all of one year his senior) was nearby in the ICU.

I went to the hospital about midnight, when things were expected to be quiet and Rob could show me around. Until about 4 A.M. there were almost no patients to be seen, and I enjoyed the chance to schmooze with my brother. I was well ready to go back to his apartment and get some sleep, though, when a patient in his forties came in by ambulance. I have no idea today what was wrong with this man, but I remember with absolute clarity what transpired in the early hours of that morning.

The man apparently had some sort of reversible lung disease, which was manifested by frequent life-threatening acute episodes, each of which, however, resolved quickly with simple medical therapy. The problem was that during the episodes he often needed to be intubated (a tube passed down into his windpipe) and placed on a ventilator. Once that was accomplished, everything would improve, and he could be sent home within a few days. The underlying condition, whatever it was, was expected to resolve gradually over a year or two, leaving this otherwise completely healthy man free to lead a long and normal life.

Standing by the cubicle in which the man was placed, I could see that he was having great difficulty breathing. I watched as my brother, after wasting very little time on a physical examination, attempted to pass the tube through his nose and into his airway. I understood this would be no easy feat for my brother, who had done it only once or twice before. I also understood that if he succeeded the man would be absolutely fine, while if he failed the man would die.

The few minutes during which Robert made his couple of attempts passed very slowly, and the man seemed to be getting worse. When the resident was called he raced past me into the room, his face almost as white as my brother's. I saw him motion toward me and ask, "Is that the son?" He was obviously relieved to find out that I wasn't.

The resident was also unable to pass the tube, the man kept turning bluer, and I could almost palpate the anxiety of my brother and his colleague. After briefly considering whether there might be any other (more manly) alternatives, they decided to wake the anesthesiologist on call, and I heard Robert quickly explain the situation over the phone. She was at home, "only" a few minutes away, but though she evidently responded at first, the line soon became silent, as if she had fallen back asleep. There was no way to reach her again, since she hadn't hung up the phone.

While Rob and the resident agonized, the patient was suffocating and beginning to lose consciousness. As for me, I felt strangely separate, as though I were an observer of something bigger than just ordinary life. Perhaps this should be a Bergman film, I kept thinking, where the appropriate ending, whether tragic or happy, would help us understand something profound, or move us to tears. But who was writing this script, and with what moral?

Suddenly the anesthesiologist dashed into the room, apologized for having momentarily dozed off, and in one motion intubated the patient. And then, almost as quickly as she'd arrived, she was gone. (Who was that masked woman?)

In an instant, with the touch of her hand, everything had changed. The patient rapidly awoke, Rob and his resident congratulated themselves on their escape from this near disaster, and I was left to ponder: life, death, careers.

It seemed such a good thing to do, this medicine. If you just mastered the skills, you could save people's lives. No muss or fuss, no deep thoughts, no complexities, subtleties, or ambiguities. Just the act of cheating death, assuming, of course, that you could do it right. Which would only require training and diligence, neither of which seemed any real obstacle at all.

Perhaps if I had known then what I know now: that physicians rarely save (really save) even a single life. That it is almost impossible to be competent, no less masterful, given the complexity of what we do. That we routinely fail despite our best efforts. That almost all our decisions are shrouded in uncertainty. That even our most perfunctory acts are troubled by extraordinary moral questions. Perhaps if I had known, I would not be writing this now.

But I didn't. And twenty-five years of medicine have given me enough experience to fill too many books. Nowhere else could I have dreamed up such a gold mine of life at its most naked—the tragedy and the comedy, the outrageous and the banal, the grace and the anguish, the courage and the terror, and even, occassionally, the joy. It's all there to borrow, if I should ever decide to become a writer after all.

JEROME R. HOFFMAN, M.D.
*Los Angeles, California*

# P A R T
# ONE

When I was a medical student at Dartmouth, a young man was brought in whose heart had stopped following a high-impact collision. I watched as the trauma surgeon "cracked" his chest by slicing a smile-shaped gash between the ribs on the left, then prying the chest open with a mechanical rib spreader that works like a car jack. The ribs popped as they were jacked apart. Within sixty seconds of starting, the surgeon had his hands inside the chest cavity, feeling for blood and massaging the heart. The young man died, but I was dazzled at this surgeon's skill.

I saw him later in the doctors' changing room. "It must be hard to learn to do that so fast and effortlessly," I said admiringly.

He looked at me sadly for a moment, and then said, "Opening the chest is the easy part. Telling the parents is the hard part."

# TRAUMA CENTER

F riday night in the South Bronx. It's the middle of
summer and the beginning of my twelve-hour
night shift in the Emergency Department of a level
one trauma center. The day had been warm, and I
knew this would mean a busy night for major
trauma. Warm days had everyone out on the streets.
Mix this with the alcohol, drugs, and handguns in
the community and you've got a violent combination.

The action began with a bang: A young man shot
in the chest over an argument about drugs was taken
to the operating room. A husband and wife who had
stabbed each other followed; he was moved into the
backup trauma room for observation of a superficial
chest injury, while she had to go to the operating
room for her abdominal stab wound. The trauma
room was just cleared when we were called by paramedics bringing in a Hispanic male with a gunshot
wound to his head. Another drug deal gone bad, I
thought, and we began to set up for his arrival.

The paramedics moved his motionless body onto

our trauma gurney. There was no spontaneous breathing or movement. He was already on a ventilator, and IVs were in place. The bullet had entered his head on the right side, just above the ear, and exited on the opposite side in nearly the same location. We monitored his blood pressure and heart rate. There wasn't much else to do.

The neurosurgical resident and I agreed we should get a CT scan of his head for completeness and then call the organ transplant team.

I left the trauma room and was writing up his chart when security informed me that the young man's family had arrived. I never get accustomed to breaking the bad news to families, but, after doing it so many times, I didn't even hesitate and headed for the small waiting room at the end of the hall. I entered the room and was surprised to find only one middle-aged man quietly sitting on the bench.

I shook his hand as we introduced ourselves. I told him I had bad news and explained the injury and the poor prognosis. After a brief pause, I asked him if he would like to see his son. He nodded, eyes closed, and said, "Take me to Louis."

We entered the trauma room where Louis was covered to midchest with a white sheet. After closing the door to the noise of the Emergency Department, the trauma room became quiet. The stillness was interrupted only by the steady swish of the respirator and the quiet beeping of the cardiac monitor. I left the room to give Mr. Ramirez time alone with his son.

Outside, I quickly sutured a patient with a scalp laceration and checked a sore throat before returning to the trauma room to bring up the question of organ donation. As I entered the room, Mr. Ramirez was kissing Louis on the forehead. He slowly turned to me and I could see the moisture in his eyes.

"Doctor," he said with a thick accent, "did you hear how this happened?"

I shook my head. I didn't know any details, but working where I did, I guessed it had to be related to drugs or a gang fight.

"Louis was on his way home from night college. He is the first one in our family to finish high school and the first one ever to go to college. He is only nineteen. He works during the day in the bodega on 149th and Third Avenue and twice a week at night he goes to City College. We are very proud of him. His mother is still in Santo Domingo with his two sisters. Only he and his fourteen-year-old brother came with me to New York. Tonight on the way home, he saw his little brother across the street fighting with some other kids. When Louis crossed the street and pulled the kids apart, one of them drew a gun and shot him. Doctor, he did nothing wrong." His voice began to crack. "Please help him."

His pleading eyes stared at me and I had to look to the floor to escape them.

"I know we don't have insurance," he said, "but here . . . maybe this will help to pay for a special test or to call in a specialist." With those words he opened a wrinkled envelope he had taken from his pocket and offered me ten one-hundred-dollar bills. "This is all the money I have saved. I have nothing else."

I gently pushed the money back to him and placed my hands on his shoulders. "I am so sorry, but there is nothing that anyone can do."

The grief welled up in him from that deep and shadowy reservoir that runs back through our ancestors. As it overtook him, it pulled his face into the contortion of crying he had probably last known when his own father died. Beneath my hands he began to physically deflate like an air mattress with the plug pulled.

Overhead, I heard an announcement about an ambulance coming in with trauma. I knew we would need the trauma room. I started to guide him back toward the waiting room. He stopped and went back to Louis. He held the young man's face in his hands. Tears now freely ran down his cheeks.

*"Adiós, hijo mío. Que Dios te acompañe."*

He touched his forehead to Louis's forehead.

I wished without hope that I would never have to feel this man's pain.

The overhead speaker: "Squad Eighty-four for Trauma One. ETA eight minutes."

I gently took Mr. Ramirez by the arm and led him away. He was now compliant. I left him in the waiting room. His younger boy was there now. A volunteer would help them through the business of death.

I went back and sat down at the nurses' station. One of the nurses told me that the ambulance was here with the victim of a gunshot wound to the abdomen. I heard myself say, "Move Ramirez to the backup trauma room and get ready for the ambulance."

My plug had been pulled too. I felt drained. So much injury to the spirit. When will it ever end?

JERRY BALLENTINE, D.O.
*New York, New York*

# ON THIN ICE

We were in the midst of an unusually busy shift in the ER when I examined a girl of sixteen or seventeen who was seated in a wheelchair. Her anxious parents had brought her in with a sprained ankle. I ordered an X ray of the ankle and said to my most aggressive and efficient nurse, Eileen, "Put some ice on the patient in room six, she's on her way to X ray." Eileen grabbed a disposable rubber glove, filled it with ice, and entered the treatment room, seemingly in one fluid motion.

Once in the room, Nurse Eileen took immediate note of the bulbous and oversize nose on my adolescent patient and slapped that ice pack right on it. "We'll get you to X ray right away," she said as she quickly moved on to her next patient.

Somewhat confused, the parents moved the ice pack from the abnormally shaped but uninjured nose and placed it on their daughter's swollen, tender ankle. Eileen, seeing this, ran back into the room, snatched the ice off the ankle, and replaced it on the now tearful patient's nose.

"Leave it there," said Eileen menacingly as she jogged off to the next patient. The family, now wondering if they had taken their pride and joy to the right hospital, quietly removed the ice pack from the cold nose and replaced it on the injured ankle.

Enter Eileen one last time. Seeing the family interfering with her attempts to ease the patient's suffering was the final straw. Eileen looked the parents right in the eyes and told them, "If you don't leave the ice where it belongs, the swelling will never go down and your daughter could end up with a funny-looking nose for the rest of her life."

MICHAEL I. GREENBERG, M.D.
*Wayne, Pennsylvania*

# EAVESDROPPING

A new intern was nervously taking a detailed history from a prim elderly woman concerning her abdominal pain. She was nearly deaf, and the questions from the intern were being relayed by this lady's grandson, who would lean over and shout in her ear. As the intern went through a long list of standardized questions, the entire ER listened in— not only to the shouted questions but also to the answers given in this nice old lady's piping voice.

Finally, in an effort to determine if the abdominal pain was from an obstructed bowel, the intern asked, "Are you passing any gas?"

The grandson dutifully leaned over and yelled in her ear, "Grandma, have you been farting?"

The old lady drew herself up and replied in a voice that penetrated every corner of the department, "Not me, must have been the doctor!"

BRADFORD L. WALTERS, M.D.
*Royal Oak, Michigan*

# BOOM

The rescue squad arrived with a twenty-eight-year-old male. He was badly bruised about the face, neck, and upper torso, with a fair amount of generalized swelling and abrasions. He was clearly despondent, and the paramedics confirmed that he was extremely depressed. Apparently he had taken an overdose of pills several hours prior to his arrival in the Emergency Department.

When asked about the type of medication he had taken, the patient admitted to using a fifth of vodka to wash down several nitroglycerin tablets in an attempt to kill himself. In response to questions about the bruises on his head and chest, he became even more despondent and described how he had repeatedly and quite forcefully rammed himself into a wall in an attempt to make the nitroglycerin explode.

ROBERT G. POWELL, M.D.
*Ashland, Virginia*

# THE CHILDREN OF
# ST. BARNARD'S

---

### CHILD ONE

I never knew the baby's name. This was not due to an oversight on my part: No one ever *gave* him a name. A pity, for the baby was a fighter and deserved better.

It happened during the mid-eighties at St. Barnard's emergency room on the South Side of Chicago. It was a rough neighborhood—and a correspondingly rough ER. If it was nasty and it happened in our neighborhood, it came to us. I remember treating paramedics bleeding from facial lacerations caused by bricks thrown through the windshields of their ambulances.

I was a moonlighting resident. I needed the money. I needed the experience even more. The Barnyard, as it was known to all other hungry residents, provided both. This particular night I felt especially blessed: We were double covered. Charlie was out of his residency, boarded, smart, and willing to teach. I remember feeling that with him behind me, the shift couldn't go wrong.

Then, they all came in at once: an unresponsive, hypothermic drunk; a screaming, bleeding man who ended up on the receiving end of a disagreement conducted with kitchen knives; a scared, hypotensive seventeen-year-old who had just delivered herself of a pregnancy she had up to now kept secret; and the seventeen-year-old's just-born baby.

Charlie and I looked at each other. Welcome to the Barnyard. "I'll take the stab wounds, you take the baby," he said. "Then you take the drunk and I'll take the mother."

The baby. My God, he was a little peanut of a thing, lying on the stretcher and gasping. I had never put a ventilation tube into the lungs of a newborn, much less a preemie. The baby laryngoscope blade barely made it in his mouth.

I said a there-are-no-atheists-in-foxholes kind of prayer, and the tube fit between the vocal cords. We had him ventilated, and we had a pulse. But the pulse was too slow for a neonate: sixty. So, we did chest compressions, and I put in an umbilical line and started pushing the drugs. I tried to guess a weight. How can you guess the weight of a smidgen-sized soul?

Still, the baby held its own. He was stabilized. Time to call the neonatologist and arrange for a transfer. They got her on the phone for me. Her first question: "How much does the baby weigh?" I didn't know. "Well, get a weight. If he's less than five hundred grams, there is no point in continuing the resuscitation. They can't survive at less than five hundred grams."

So we all stood around and stared at our baby, the baby we had got back from death, while the nurses rounded up a nursery scale. It felt like the whole ER staff stood there as I lowered him onto the scale. The neonatologist stayed on the line, and even Charlie strayed in, having single-handedly saved everyone else in the department in the meantime.

Less than five hundred grams. Not even close enough that I could fake it. A roomful of faces fell simultaneously. "Just pull the tube and forget about it," said my neonatologist. Easy for her to say. She wasn't looking at the kid. I hung up and walked over to the baby, turned off the line, pulled the tube from the lungs. In my naïveté, I thought that would be the hard part. We all stood there, mute, watching him.

He kept breathing.

"He'll stop soon," I said. "Let's get back to the others." Disconsolate, we all shuffled out. My drunk was on a warming blanket. His temp was up. We told the mother about her baby. She didn't care. I wrote up a couple of charts, and then looked over to the room.

He was still breathing.

And he kept on breathing. Dear Lord, was the scale wrong? If I, like a fool, rushed back in and reintubated the kid, wouldn't I just be resuscitating someone with severe brain injury? I gritted my teeth, and wrote up another chart. I looked over again.

Still breathing.

Word began to spread. First, it was a few ward clerks who came and stood in a circle around the stretcher. The next time I glanced over, it was some nuns. One chart later, and a collection of paramedics stood there. Then, some beat cops. No one gawked. No one spoke. All had seen life wasted, wasted daily, wasted badly. They had numbed themselves to that pain. This was somehow worse. This little baby did not want to waste his only chance. He struggled, and struggled, heart continuing to beat at the too-slow rate of sixty, chest muscles continuing to try to draw air into fluid-filled lungs.

I noticed that the policemen had their hats off.

I couldn't stand to keep looking over there. I vanished to suture a long laceration. When I returned, my eyes were drawn inexorably to the room. His room. To my relief, it was empty. It was over. Now they could take his little body to the morgue, or the funeral home, or wherever they put small dead people who gave life their best shot.

I looked down at my chart. A large plastic bag was in front of me with the now dead baby sealed inside.

It was labeled TISSUE SPECIMEN FOR PATHOLOGY.

I never knew the baby's name. They never gave him one. A pity. He deserved better.

## CHILD TWO

He had a handsome face. I could see that, even though half of it looked like mush.

He was fifteen years old. He came in with his mother, a quiet woman, who sat patiently by his side. He had tripped while playing basketball and fallen onto the jagged edge of the Cyclone fence, ripping open the left side of his face.

The wound was awful: stellate, deep, and with enough twists and turns, flaps and layers to challenge a plastic surgeon. This was out of my league. This required someone with more expertise than I had. I was going to have to get the plastic surgeon on call. Foolishly, I told the mother that. Then I called the plastic surgeon.

"Medicaid patient? I'm not coming in for that," he said.

"But it's his face," I pleaded. "He has to wear that face for the rest of his life!"

"Transfer him to Cook County. An intern will stitch him up there."

"That's just it. That's all he'd get: an intern. I can do a better job than an intern and I don't think I can do a good enough job."

"I'm not coming in for a Medicaid."

"But you're the plastic surgeon on call. You've got to come in and take these cases on your call days. Besides," I added, foolishly trying to reach a heart that wasn't there, "it's his face!"

"I'm sick of Medicaid, sick of endless paperwork, hostile bureaucrats, mindless lawsuits, and no pay. Medicaid is a joke. I'm not coming in."

"I'll call the hospital administrator. You are obliged to come."

The plastic surgeon, who must have taken the Hippocratic oath at some point in his life, blew up. "I'm retiring at the end of the month. I'll call the hospital administrator and submit my resignation right now. I'm not coming!" He hung up.

I was stuck. No other plastic surgeon would come in. They were not on call. I went back in to face the mother. She took the news calmly. I told her that I was not the best person for the job. I told her that I would do the best I could. I told her that it was her choice: I could transfer him to Cook. She might find someone better there.

She looked at her son's beautiful face. No, she said. She would take a chance on me.

I did my best, but that's all I can say. I still think of him, now. I wonder what he is doing, down on the South Side of Chicago with a mother who loves him and half a beautiful face.

## CHILD THREE

He did not have a beautiful face. It was all doughy and acne scarred. It didn't help matters that his eyes were two red puffs and his mouth was held in the rigid contortion of trying not to cry. At eleven, he was almost as big as the cop who brought him in.

"We just need to confirm the abuse," said the cop, looking equal parts embarrassed and bored. "We'll take the pictures down at the station."

The boy had called the police himself. He called not to report his own abuse, which was of long duration. That was evident. The scars on his back and chest and legs were classic electric-cord whip injuries: the narrow hairpin loop marks that look a bit like a brand. He had hundreds of scars of different ages. I could see the shiny, flat, well-healed ones that he probably got at six. The scars that were still red were acquired at age ten. The fresh ones looked less than a week old.

He had not called to report this. He had called because, on this day, his mother had started to beat his younger brother.

He sat there silently crying. He cried because he felt rotten. He sobbed because he had turned in his mother. He cried for his little brother. He cried for himself.

I wrote up the chart. I went to the vending room and got some microwave popcorn. I brought him the bag. We sat together eating the popcorn, he and I, and I felt as I watched him munch in silence that I was wrong. He had one of the most beautiful faces I had ever seen.

TRACEY GOESSEL, M.D.
*Hunt Valley, Maryland*

*Like ripe fall fruit from a wild apple tree, babies tumble from the wombs of careless and innocent un-noticing young mothers. In contrast is the agony and yearning of the barren and infertile woman. And when the mind is weakened by mental illness, the power of this deep and primitive reproductive urge becomes seen as it forces its way up into the light of daily behavior.*

# THE WISH

In an upper-income community hospital Emergency Department, a fifty-year-old matron complained of mild abdominal pain and fever. The patient was on an antidepressant, but she had no other significant medical history. Her physical exam was unremarkable. Lab tests did little to further the diagnosis. I decided to proceed with a pelvic exam. A female nurse set the patient up in the GYN room.

As I approached the room, the nurse shook her head in disbelief suggesting we were getting close to a diagnosis. The pelvic exam revealed that the patient's labia were pinned together with three large, rusty safety pins.

The patient apparently had a long psychiatric history, including obsessive behavior focused on her inability to bear children. Two weeks earlier, the patient had purchased a small chicken at the market and had inserted it, piece by piece, into her vagina. She had pinned her labia to keep the chicken in place and was waiting for it to develop into a baby.

The patient was subsequently admitted to the psych unit, but not before she was washed out with two liters of Betadine douche and the entire chicken carcass was accounted for.

GREGORY DAVID POST, M.D.
*New York, New York*

# EVIDENCE COLLECTION IN
# THE EMERGENCY ROOM

She is a 13-year-old waif,
with a 16-year-old body,
and a lifetime of cares.

And as I pluck ten hairs from her head
(with the roots),
and scrape whatever I can find from under her
    fingernails,
and comb her pubic hairs into the envelope,
and take the pictures,
and write down the story,
with details about her mental state,
and how she cried,
and trembled,
and seemed believable,
I wonder.

How a father could do this to a daughter,
his drunkenness notwithstanding.
And I wonder

how a mother could be in such denial,
her marriage notwithstanding.

And I wonder how a 13-year-old child
can ever survive such a violation
to her childness,
and her humanness.

And where will she be in ten years?
Or twenty?
And what kind of life will she have?
And her children?
And her children's children?

And I wonder if I'll ever get used to this.
And if I do,
will I still like myself?

KEITH N. BYLER, D.O.
*Edwardsville, Illinois*

# THE UNEXPECTED MIRACLE

It's the usual Friday night scene in a county hospital Emergency Department. All that remains of another drive-by shooting victim is splotches of blood on my shoes. A swearing, spitting drug abuser is held down by security guards while being placed in four-point restraint. Quiet crying comes from behind the curtain hiding a woman who has painful gallstones. A young AIDS patient stares hauntingly from sunken eyes, his gaunt face distorted by the purple blotches of Kaposi's sarcoma. Three patients with their EMT entourage lie on gurneys by the door, like planes waiting to land, vainly hoping for an empty bed. All around the room are the sullen, resigned faces of those who have waited up to twenty-four hours to be seen for their sore throats or sprained ankles. The stench of an unwashed homeless man in the corner, ravenously consuming a brown-bag hospital-issue lunch, permeates the atmosphere. Walls display reminders of the season: cardboard candy canes, blinking minilights, and grinning Santas bearing sacks of gifts, the likes of which no patient in this department will see.

In the midst of the chaos, I hear the manic chatter of a giddily cheerful middle-aged woman. She greets everyone in passing with a jolly "Merry Christmas" and an endless stream of meandering conversation. She is in the Emergency Department for a chronic infection in her lower legs. While I examine her, she talks on about living on the streets, peppering her narrative with references to life before homelessness. Her eyes take on a sparkle as she describes her prior home: two stories, five bedrooms, three-car garage. Her unwashed hair falls in clumps across her forehead as she proudly speaks of three successful sons. She describes her husband, a prosperous banker, handsome as a movie star. A shadow crosses her face when the nurse asks where her husband and sons are now. After a pause, she ignores the question and continues her chronicle.

Her lofty tales extend to her own life. She boasts of being a Juilliard scholar, of playing violin in New York City's philharmonic. Her hands wave grandly as she describes standing ovations, velvet curtains, black satin dresses, and postperformance parties. We humor her with tolerant smiles and give one another knowing glances. As she is wheeled from the room, she beams magnificently and promises to come back to play her violin for us. We nod patronizingly, then forget as we turn to yet another patient in need.

A week later, the scene is the same. More sullen faces, another psychotic patient screaming incessantly, more shooting victims, more pain, more endless need. Patients and staff alike are stretched to the limits of tolerance. Doctors snap at clerks, patients swear at nurses. A general murmur of discontent pervades. I feel pulled in all directions at once, working as fast as I can while falling more and more behind.

No one notices her come into the room. No one notices her take the rolling stool and position herself in a doorway. No one notices her take out the violin, place the cloth to her chin, and rest her cheek gently against the instrument. No one notices her raise her right arm and carefully place the bow to the strings.

The first pure, sweet notes drift softly into the confusion, taking everyone by surprise. Out of her violin flows phrase after phrase of perfect sound. Her musical repertoire is as disjointed as her conversation: a bit of Bach, a few show tunes, a little Gershwin, Mozart interspersed with carols of the season. Her technique reflects the Juilliard years. Her face is composed, peaceful, almost beautiful. I wonder if her mind is in another time, a time of black satin dresses, handsome husbands, and loving sons.

Her concert lasts four continuous hours, no musical phrase ever repeating itself. The first person affected is the psychotic man. He becomes quiet, pauses to hear her music. Patients waiting in chairs listen intently. When their conversations resume, frowns are eased and they chat amiably in hushed voices. Two patients stop weeping, their attention drawn to the music. The staff members slow their pace a fraction, and smiles replace the angry tension in their faces. I find myself humming snatches of music I recognize. A calmness settles on the Emergency Department, muting the continuing bustle. Peaceful feelings of the holiday blossom and, for four hours, tranquillity reigns.

The last note hangs in the air as she lowers her arms and looks around the room. She blushes, startled out of her reverie by the faces focused on her, and carefully places the violin back in its case. She stands slowly, shuffles over to me on her painful, swollen legs, and murmurs, "I just wanted to thank you." Having worked her magic, she departs quietly, leaving me in awe of the unexpected beauty and dignity of life.

DIANE BIRNBAUMER, M.D.
*Lomita, California*

# P A R T
# TWO

When I was an intern at San Francisco General, a bag lady came in saying she was falling down on occasion. Since she was in her sixties, we worried about heart problems or transient strokes. She reported no other medical problems or symptoms.

We helped her undress, which took time because she was a mummy of clothing layers interspersed with layers of newspaper. When we got down to the last layer and uncovered her leg, it was alive with thousands of maggots wriggling in what was left of her flesh.

I felt a visceral stun. There was a moment where my brain could not absorb the information my eyes were sending to it. It had to make some adjustment before moving on.

I think of this now as I watch a coworker bite a doughnut while working on a mutilated trauma victim, and I wonder if as the bizarre becomes commonplace there is a hidden cost to the self.

# PART
# TWO

# MAN'S BEST FRIEND

On a clear, crisp Sunday morning in late June, we were ready to end our shift in the trauma unit. The call schedule at Cook County Hospital runs twenty-four hours, but the summer months seem to tug and pull until they blur into a long stretch of gunshot wounds, broken bones, and assaults.

We were waiting for the morning report when the call came in: A stab wound was coming up the elevator to the trauma suite. The door crashed open and the paramedics stood there with a bloody mound of angry sheets twisting on their cot. They rolled into the room, followed by police, ambulance attendants, and hospital staff. They huddled around the cot and, with shouts and awkward laughter, heaved the body over on to the trauma cart.

It was a drunk.

He was out of it and could barely answer questions. His vitals were stable, but even now there was a fine spray of blood and fluid arcing up and out of him.

He had no penis.

He lived alone in a rooming house with a ratty little poodle. He had a history of both alcoholism and depression. The night before, he had gotten drunk and gone to the kitchen in search of a knife. He found one, a big carving knife, and used it to saw off his penis and testicles. Then he staggered in to the bathroom, trailing blood and urine along the way, and ran the blade into the bathroom wall through a photo of his mother.

He reeked of stool and urine and beer. He was in his mid-fifties but looked ten years older. His hair was caked off to one side with grime, and a thick stubble erupted around a mouth of peglike teeth. He kept trying to say his name but could only manage a whispered slur. He denied any pain or injury. The bleeding was stopped with pressure, and the urologist was called to the ER. After examination, he thought surgical reattachment might be successful, depending on the condition of the genitals.

The paramedics had not brought in the body parts, so the police were dispatched to recover them.

An officer soon returned. Somewhat out of breath, he began his report:

"In twenty years on the force, I've never seen nothing like this. The apartment was filled with stench and garbage. The little mutt was yappin' and runnin' around and bitin' at our ankles. Blood and urine was everywhere: on the floor, on the walls, on the kitchen table. But nowhere could we find the guy's pecker. All of a sudden I hear this gagging sound and I look over in the corner and this little mutt is choking up the guy's pecker. The dog had eaten it."

To prove it, he held up a McDonald's sandwich bag and took out a shredded penis and scrotum, testicles bobbing like yo-yos, chewed up and covered with saliva and hair.

The patient recovered and was taught to pee sitting down. After he was discharged a week later, we'd occasionally see him staggering down the street, his head in a cloud of wine. The cop went back on patrol, and even won a commendation from his precinct for medical assistance.

No one knows what happened to little Fifi.

BLAINE HOUMES, M.D.
*Cedar Rapids, Iowa*

# GOT MILK?

I was working in the trauma area of Detroit Receiving Hospital. I was a third-year emergency medicine resident. A young black woman was sitting quietly on the stretcher, waiting to be seen.

"Hi, I'm Dr. Vassallo. What's the problem tonight?"

"I've been shot in the head." She said it matter-of-factly, indifferently.

"You look good for having been shot in the head," I said.

"I've been shot in the head," she said again. This time she elaborated nonchalantly: "I was on my way to Kentucky Fried Chicken and somebody shot me in the head."

"Where are you shot?" I asked. She pointed to a spot on the back of her head. I touched it with my finger and felt an almost imperceptible laceration through her thick hair.

"OK, we'll get an X ray and see," I said.

I returned a little later. "You're lucky," I said. "You *have* been shot in the head. The bullet is flat like a pancake against the bone of the skull. But it didn't go in or even crack your skull." I reported this enthusiastically.

"I drink a lot of milk," she said.

At that moment her friends joined her at the bedside. They had all been together when the whole thing occurred. Hoping to get a reaction, I announced that their friend had been shot in the head and it was a wonder she hadn't been injured.

"We know she was shot in the head. That's why we brought her here," they said. "It's her birthday today."

With everything explained, they went home.

SUSI VASSALLO, M.D.
*New York, New York*

# TREASURE HUNT

A morbidly obese woman was brought to the Emergency Department for shortness of breath on a tarp dragged by six firemen. After positioning two gurneys side by side, we somehow managed to lift her up. She was in respiratory failure due to her weight, which we estimated to be approximately five hundred pounds.

Attempting to undress her, we lifted her arms up to pull her very large blouse over her head. To our surprise, an asthma inhaler fell out from under her right armpit. It had been enveloped in the skin.

Reviewing her chest X ray, we noticed a round density in the left chest. With the help of an assistant, we lifted up her massive left breast to find a shiny dime. No telling how long it had been there.

Finally, a nurse and two technicians attempted to place a Foley catheter in her bladder. After spreading apart one tree-trunk leg at a time, they found a handful of industrial paper towels, apparently being used as a sanitary napkin. But they also found an even bigger surprise in her crotch—a TV remote control.

When I gave a report about the patient to the unhappy admitting physician, I tried to cheer him up by reminding him that if he did a thorough exam, he too could find buried treasure. We nicknamed our patient The Human Couch.

The patient's family was very happy that we found the remote.

WILLIAM MALONEY, M.D.
*Evanston, Illinois*

# ODE TO A JOHN DOE

An old man walked out the front door of his house on a lazy, sunny Sunday afternoon, looked back at his wife, and said, *"Ahorita regreso, mi vieja. Voy a traerte tu comida favorita."* ("I'll be back in a minute, honey. I'll get you your favorite food.") He started down the street to their favorite seafood restaurant. The warm sun felt good on his face. His arthritis was not hurting him and he had not been to the hospital for chest pains in six months. He was eighty-seven and thoughtful about his health.

As he reached the busy intersection, the first car stopped for him and he took it as a signal to walk across the street. After several steps he looked again to check on the car in the next lane. As he turned his head, the thud of car hitting human was heard—the muffled sound of bones giving way as the car struck him and sent him through the air.

That same afternoon, I was entertaining friends at home. As we began eating, my phone rang. It was Lourdes, a nurse from the ER where I work.

"Doctor Lopez, sorry to disturb you but your aunt

is here looking for your grandfather. He went out for food over two hours ago and has not returned. When your aunt went to the restaurant she heard that an old man had been in accident and she came here. He's not here, but I heard that a traumatic full arrest was taken to L.A. County Hospital." A tingling came over me. As I thanked her and hung up the phone, I felt the strange weight of death.

"What's wrong?" asked my friend Jorge.

"My grandfather is missing. He may have been involved in an accident. There is a John Doe at L.A. County. It could be him. I'm sorry, but I have to go."

Jorge drove me to the hospital. On our way there, I talked to him about Grandpa. He had come here at the age of ten with his mother and father. By seventeen he had begun working for Sunkist, and he stayed with them until he retired as a plant supervisor at sixty-five. He met my grandmother when they were youngsters working in the fields. Her father would not let him marry her until he had saved eight hundred dollars. They had children, grandchildren, and great-grandchildren. When I was admitted to medical school, he gave me tuition money from his savings. When I told him I would pay him back, he waved me off and said, "You will pay me back when you do the same for your children."

When we arrived at the Emergency Department, I introduced myself to the chief resident there, who told me about the John Doe as she walked me to the trauma room. "Elderly Hispanic male in traumatic full arrest with massive head injuries, multiple lower extremity and rib fractures. We got back a blood pressure but it's shaky. Right now he's comatose, has a blood pressure of sixty, two large-bore needles going full speed, two chest tubes, and a clean abdominal tap."

As we walked into the room, my eyes scanned the

bruised, splinted, swollen legs and the exposed chest full of tubes and wires, still hoping that it might not be Grandpa. I looked up to see the face. The intubated, swollen, bloodied head with scant grayish hair took seconds to come into focus. I knew that this mangled John Doe was my grandfather. The resident's voice became distant, and all I could hear were the rhythmic noise of the respirator, the beeps of the monitor, the shuffling sounds of people around him.

My voice was tight as I talked to the resident and the attending physician.

"I am afraid you have been much too skilled for my grandfather's good. You have done a wonderful job, but if he goes into another cardiac arrest, please let him go. He is eighty-seven years old and has had a good life."

Grandpa died a few minutes later.

I thanked the doctors and went to call my family. When I came back to see Grandpa, his body had been covered with a white sheet and moved aside. In his place there was another full arrest being worked on. John Doe number one was making way for John Doe number two.

I did not want my family to see him here and in this way. I wanted a place of quiet and privacy for this final meeting.

I asked the charge nurse if she could help. She told me how sorry she was and gave me a hug. Then she found an empty booth where my family could view Grandpa with some privacy. She helped me clean his bloody, battered body. She also called in a priest to give him the last rites. After seeing a thousand shattered families, she could still care.

When Grandma arrived, she asked me, *"Cómo está mi esposo?"* ("How is my husband?") I told her with a hoarse, whispering voice: *"Lo atropelló un carro y se murió, Abuelita."* ("A car ran him over and killed him, Grandma.") Her wrinkled face aged even more and she let out a long, sorrowful cry. I led her down to the booth where Grandpa's body was waiting. She touched his face and said, *"Esta muy frío."* ("He's very cold.") She was crying and kissed him. I lost my composure and hugged my mother and grand-mother as we cried and cried. It was an emotional catharsis that as a doctor I never allow myself. In this grief I was able to retrieve some of the feeling that I had become insulated from in the role of phy-sician.

A priest came and gathered the family for prayers. A visible sense of calm came into Grandma's face as we prayed together. After a short while, we took her home and made all the preparations to retrieve Grandpa's body. A few days later, hundreds of peo-ple came to remember him, and the line of cars that accompanied the funeral procession stretched for several blocks.

When I look back at this painful experience, one thing stands out. I will always remember the nurse who helped me start the painful process of grieving. Her kindness helped remind me to reach out from my heart to the survivors of the dead. I will always remember that a John Doe is somebody's father, brother, or grandfather. Even my own.

AL LOPEZ, M.D.
*Los Angeles, California*

# EL HOWIE

I was a fourth-year medical student rotating through an academic Emergency Department in the southwestern United States. There was a first-year resident, Howie, from the Midwest, who was struggling to learn Spanish. Spanish did not come easily to him, but that didn't stop him from attempting to communicate with Spanish-speaking patients. Howie was one who believed that any lack of skill could be masked by a loud, authoritative voice.

One lazy Saturday afternoon, a car drove up to the Emergency entrance. A young man ran into the Emergency Department screaming, in Spanish, that his wife was having a baby. Also in the car were several soon-to-be grandparents. Howie, hoping for a delivery, ran to the car and found the head of the baby beginning to show. He positioned himself between the mother's legs, among a sea of grandparents, and urged her to push by yelling, *"Puta! Puta! Puta!"* The grandmother began to cry and the husband needed to be restrained.

What Howie was trying to say was *"Puja!"*

("Push!") Instead, to this young woman who was delivering her first baby in the backseat of a car, he was yelling, "Whore! Whore! Whore!"

THOMAS MOTYCKA, M.D.
*Columbia, South Carolina*

# NOT EVER

I was finishing up an unusually busy Thursday shift. Seven patients had been brought in all at once from a car accident. Fortunately, the injuries were minor, but the paperwork had kept me busy until two hours beyond my 3 P.M. changeover time. Finally, I finished. Just before I headed out the door, one of the nurses called me to the phone. "An emergency," she said.

"Emergency." In no other setting could that word be so overused. The nurse's grim expression puzzled me as I reached for the phone with my left hand, my right holding my white coat slung over my shoulder.

"Philip?" my wife's voice sobbed. "I think our daughter has been killed."

*"What?"* My knees buckled as my shout reverberated around the large chamber.

During my wife's dance lesson, our four-year-old, Lauren, had wandered away from the child care area. She had been found in the otherwise unoccupied weight room, asphyxiated by a two-hundred-pound bench press she had dislodged across her chest.

Two good friends from the nursing staff drove me to the medical center where the ambulance had taken my sweet baby. I refused to fantasize. Lauren's condition was critical, but I knew so little that I concentrated on good thoughts and hopes. Tears rolled down my cheeks.

On my arrival, I was led to the "quiet room," which is reserved for grieving families, to join my weeping wife. I do not like quiet rooms. I needed to be with my daughter. My daughter needed me with her. My wife needed me to be with my daughter, too, for she could not.

"The doctor told me that if she recovers, she's going to be brain damaged," she said. "Did I do the wrong thing to bring her back?" My wife had just finished recertifying in CPR training the week before and had administered CPR until the ambulance arrived.

"No," I insisted. "No one can tell what will result."

A nurse led me into the trauma room where the pediatric surgeon was having difficulty starting the arterial line. Lauren had been completely limp when she arrived in the Emergency Department. Now I noted that she was responding to the painful stimulus with primitive reflexive posturing. I pulled up a stool, stationing myself by her side, and held her hand. For the next two hours I sat there, calling to her gently, telling her stories, singing her songs. Lauren's favorite song had always been "You Are My Sunshine." Every time I came to the last line I became too choked to produce it. Rhythmically, the ventilator went up and down.

Over the next few hours Lauren showed small signs of improvement, and by 11 P.M. we had all moved to her room in the neurological intensive care unit.

Our friends rallied to our needs. Through the evening and throughout the night, visitors brought comforting words, gifts, and good wishes. The magic and power of all our hopes permeated the room. Lauren continued to show good signs. At two in the morning she reached up and scratched her scalp. I rejoiced. At the very least she would have self-care.

Then, at 4 A.M., our miracle bloomed. Lauren opened her eyes and, around the endotracheal tube, mouthed "What happened?" Tears, laughter, the rejoicing of redemption filled our room.

Later that morning, an astonished neurosurgeon gave permission for removal of the ET tube. Within an hour, Lauren had wiggled her arms free enough to disconnect all her other tubes. Late that night Lauren was transferred to the pediatric ward, and the next day she and her dozen new dollies piled into the wheelchair and rolled out the door.

Every day I see patients who recover, and all too often I deal with the families of those who die. Yesterday, a fifteen-year-old boy was brought in with a head injury sustained in a car accident. His mother stood in tears at his side, holding his hand and calling softly to his unresponsive limpness. I would like to have said, "I know how you feel." But no one ever can. Not even now.

PHILIP L. LEVIN, M.D.
*Browns Summit, North Carolina*

# MAKING SENSE

It is rare that I suffer for my patients anymore, and I almost never do while I am actually in the ER working. Sometimes when I'm home, hours later, I remember the weeping parents of a child who drowned, and let myself feel, if just for a moment, the smallest visceral pain. Not for the child, whom I never really see as a living person. But for all of us: the parents, the baby-sitter, myself, my own children . . .

I tend to take solace, though, in the thought that with greater vigilance things like this might not happen. Not that I'm judgmental: I do care about my patients even when they're alcoholics or junkies; I understand the pain of the mother whose son was shot holding up a store, the terror of the chronic lunger gasping for breath after years of smoking, the helpless rage of the hemophiliac with a now worthless knee after he played in a game of soccer, when he knew he shouldn't. And it isn't that I haven't done all these same things in my own way, for I have.

43

But still, there is some comfort when you can find a reason for tragedy, a defect of character that changes, even a little bit, an innocent victim into someone who had it coming. Maybe it makes the daily onslaught of misery seem just the tiniest bit less cruel. Or maybe it merely lets me feel safer myself.

One night at about 1 A.M. the paramedics brought in a twenty-five-year-old man from an auto accident. His BMW was destroyed, and he was comatose, with vital signs that were preterminal. I knew without even thinking about it that he was going to die. Such knowledge always makes resuscitations run smoothly; there's no frantic behavior when you know nothing you do can harm a patient.

What I noticed most about this patient, while members of the trauma team stripped him of his trendy outfit and started IVs and hooked up monitors, was how serene he looked in the midst of all this activity. And what a striking specimen he was. He had the physique of an athlete, or a model. Even his tan was just right. I also noticed the odor of alcohol when he breathed. Not overwhelming, but undeniable. To me, it was like a breath of fresh air.

Running a trauma code involves doing many things at once, but I managed in the next few minutes to develop a clear picture in my own mind of this man who was going to die so young and who, for all the tragedy of it, I knew with a great bone weariness, had done this to himself. Like many another Southern Californian, I was sure, he had been blessed with too much: youth, looks, money, the time to work out, preen, and strut. And now, driving drunk after a late night out, he had killed himself. I only hoped that the driver in the other car wasn't hurt too bad. (Though I felt in my gut he would be, I comforted myself with the thought that, at least according to the statistics, there was an awfully good chance he'd been drunk too.)

By the time the patient's heart stopped, after our multiple interventions had failed, several of his friends had made their way to the waiting room. Here's what they, and the half dozen or so others who slowly streamed in throughout the night, had to tell me.

The patient had moved to L.A. one month before, after graduating at the top of his class at a prestigious law school. He had been hired by a top law firm in town, and was driving home from the celebratory dinner they threw for him when the accident occurred. He'd had a beer with dinner, apparently, and another not too long before leaving, but they were certain he hadn't drunk anything stronger. (In fact, the blood level ultimately came back close to zero.) We also later found out from the police that an eyewitness had said the other vehicle, a van, had suddenly swerved into the young man's car, hitting him head on. I never did find out if that driver was in fact drunk, or how bad he was injured.

The patient's older brother, tall like the patient but skinny, with scraggly hair and wearing old jeans, told me he himself was the black sheep of the family, a struggling artist, while his brother was the golden boy. Although he'd always wished his parents would be just as proud of him, he'd never really resented his brother—how could you resent someone so generous and loving? An ex-girlfriend said she'd never respected a man so much, and still considered him her best friend, even though the romance hadn't worked out. A couple of new colleagues from work said this guy was amazing— so bright and yet so easygoing and noncompetitive. The current girlfriend was merely inconsolable.

Usually I try to avoid giving terrible news over

the phone, but his parents lived in St. Louis. When I woke the father it was about 4:30 A.M. their time. After I said I was calling from California with some very bad news, there was silence. And there was more silence as I described the accident, and then more as I went over all we had tried to do. I went slowly, hoping to be gentle but direct, trying to allow him to ask any questions before he heard "dead" and excluded any other input, trying to say the things people like to hear about "not feeling pain" and "happening quickly," wanting not to keep him in suspense but also to cushion the blow, wishing I would be able use my words to do for him what an arm around the shoulder sometimes does, and, finally, dreading the terror and pain and rage he would feel, and which he might direct back at me, the messenger. When I was done, after what seemed like a very long speech, uninterrupted by sounds from the other end of the phone two thousand miles away, there was a bit more silence, and then the father said: "So what are you telling me?" And then I heard him say to his wife, "This is someone from California. There's been an accident. Ask him what he's saying."

I was on the phone with them, on and off, for much of the rest of the night, and though they clearly knew that their son was dead, they never really seemed to understand, each in turn asking from time to time "So what happened?" or "What exactly are you saying?" or "You're a doctor from California?" I never talked to them again, after that night, and I don't know if they could ever make sense of what had happened. I certainly couldn't.

JEROME R. HOFFMAN, M.D.
*Los Angeles, California*

# CONTINUITY OF CARE

R esidency interviews are a nightmare. I sit there
  in my interview suit complete with tie. Do I look
too conservative? Not conservative enough? A riv-
ulet of sweat inches down to my boxers while the
man behind the desk rifles through my file, searching for something: a flaw or an interesting tidbit.
Eventually he sits forward and with a level gaze
poses the question: "Why do you want to practice
emergency medicine?"

An honest answer would be, "I'm not entirely sure
why, sir. Perhaps you, as a practicing emergency
physician, could tell me." But instead I launch into
my well-rehearsed oration on the benefits of emergency medicine as a career. I am careful to include all
the catchphrases: opportunity to treat a variety of
medical complaints, to bring primary care to the
underserved, to have a flexible, pager-free lifestyle . . .

If my answer has not left the interviewer comatose, he may counter with, "Well, don't you think
you'll miss the continuity of care that primary practice offers?" To this I assert that emergency medicine

has its own continuity, and that emergency physicians can follow a patient's course both in and out of the hospital. Sometimes, if I feel relaxed, I tell this story:

It was an unusual day in Seattle. The sun was shining over the city. I was enjoying my first day off in three weeks of a surgical rotation, walking along the street carrying a Nordstrom's bag containing a salmon and some vegetables from the Public Market. A distressed teenage girl was stopped on the sidewalk. Next to the business-lunch crowd who were studiously avoiding her, I'm sure I looked like the country cousin shopping in the big city.

The girl came to me and plaintively asked, "Sir, can you help me?" She wore a black-and-white houndstooth overcoat and her clothes had a lived-in look. Her face was a harsh mosaic of bruises and abrasions masked with eyeliner, blusher, and lipstick applied with questionable skill.

I was about to ignore her plea when something caught my eye. I stopped. "Sure, what can I do for you?"

"Thank God," she exclaimed, turning her head to the sunlight in an obviously practiced gesture. "Finally, somebody who will listen to me." Listen was all I could do for the next few minutes as she told me her story with the rapidity of a telemarketer. Her name was Cathy. She was a high school senior from Chehalis. Her parents were visiting relatives in Iowa, leaving her alone at home under the lax supervision of the neighbors. She had come to Seattle yesterday to go shopping. Somehow she had become separated from her friends, and had walked across town, hoping to meet them at the bus station. A gang of kids had beaten her and taken the purse with her money and return bus ticket. She had spent last night curled up behind a dumpster, afraid that she was going to

be murdered or raped. She hadn't had anything to
eat since yesterday, and she didn't think she would
last another night on the street. No, she hadn't contacted the police, because she was afraid her parents
would find out that she had left town against their
strict admonitions. She feared they would ground
her forever. Yes, she had tried to call friends in Chehalis, but no one was home. She was really just a
good kid that had made a bad decision, and if she
ever made it back to Chehalis alive, she would never
leave again without her parents' permission.

"All I need is twenty-seven dollars for a bus ticket
back home. You can even walk me to the station and
watch me buy the ticket." Her eyes darted back and
forth between my face and the Nordstrom's bag.

She thought that I had stopped in deference to her
vulnerability. In fact, it was a five-centimeter red
crescent above her left eye that had caught my attention. In the crescent were eighteen size 6-0 Prolene sutures. I knew that below the Prolene were
four more of Vicryl. I had stopped to admire my
suturing handiwork. Not bad for a third-year student, I thought.

"As soon as I get back to Chehalis, I'll mail you
your money," she continued. "I can even wire it to
you if you want. I'll pay you back. Honest. I prom-
ise."

Sometime during a blur of bad coffee and late
nights, the surgery intern and I had been called
down to the ER to help sew up drunks with head
lacerations. When I showed up, the trauma doc had
grunted and pointed down the hall at a gurney holding a restrained figure with a pillowcase for a head.
She had been spitting blood at the staff. The chart
had listed her name as Krystal, and she had been
delivered by a police unit returning from a domestic
violence call. Her medical history read: "None of

your fucking business, you donkey-faced homo." As I cleaned the blood from her hair and face, she spewed forth with a continuous diatribe about my supposed sexual orientation toward animal species and humans of both sexes. Giving her a local anesthetic was a tough battle despite my advantages of height and weight.

Suturing of the wound would have been dangerous to us both were it not for a passing nurse who procured a mirror and appealed to Krystal's vanity. "If you don't hold still and let the boy do a good job of stitching that up, you're going to look like you chase parked cars in your spare time."

Krystal lay still and silent for the forty-five minutes it took me to close her wound. As I finished, the intern returned to chide me for using too many sutures and to take me back upstairs. I had not been responsible for her discharge instructions, but looking at the ten-day-old wound, I knew that she had not kept her follow-up appointment for suture removal.

"Even if you could just give me a ten or a twenty, I'd be that much closer to home," she implored sweetly.

"OK," I distractedly mumbled, "let's go to the bus station." Again she thanked God. The walk to the Greyhound terminal was short. I preferred her previous obscenities to her current saccharine effluence. As we neared the window, she held out a hand for money to buy the ticket. When I pulled out a credit card, she became suddenly tense.

"They don't take credit cards here."

"The little sign says they do."

"Well, maybe they do, but they don't like it," she warned.

"They'll get over it."

"There's a bank machine around the corner; you

could just get the cash and wouldn't have to use your card."

The apathetic woman in the window ignored our dialogue and asked, "Where are you folks going today?"

I turned to the girl, "Well, where do you want to go, since you know you can't cash the ticket the moment I walk out?"

"Bastard!" She pivoted and stormed out.

"Sorry." I shrugged to the cashier, and left.

She was walking slowly back up the sidewalk. I matched her gait. "Get the fuck away from me or I'll scream."

"When was the last time you ate?"

"What do you care?"

"I care. Why don't you let me buy you lunch and take the stitches out of your face?" Her hand came up and her ring finger worried one of the tiny blue filaments at her brow. She stared at me. "Can you do that?"

"Why not? I put them in." She looked surprised.

We sat at the counter and she wolfed three hamburgers. Between bites she told me a different story. Her name was Christine, and she was from Moses Lake. Her father taught shop and coached football at the high school where she had been a junior. Her mother sold cosmetics, and spent the rest of her time "trying to ruin my life." She couldn't stand the farm-boy jocks her parents wanted her to date. She found school tedious and frustrating, and her sharp tongue landed her on probation all too frequently. She'd run away from home with her boyfriend, an older, notorious, small-town coke dealer with a black Trans Am. They were going to make the big time: live in a nice house, own a ski boat, and throw wild parties for all their friends. They'd laugh at the hicks living back in Moses Lake. The competition in the city cocaine trade had proved too much for her friend, however, and soon he was sampling more than he was selling. One morning, after the money ran out, her boyfriend slapped her around and pushed her from their room. She was to come back with a hundred dollars or not come back at all.

It took her four days. She had tried begging, stealing, and selling herself. She had been beaten twice; once by a territorial prostitute and once by a man demanding a refund when she choked. Finally, a kind soul had befriended her and bought her a bus ticket to Moses Lake. She cashed the ticket in. Over the next several months the cycle was repeated. The bus ticket scam became more polished. The beatings and demands for money became more frequent.

"Sometimes I wish I'd've just taken that first ticket and gone back to Moses Lake," was her lament.

"Why don't you go now?"

"I've been a whore and lived with a drug dealer. My parents would never take me back. They'd kill me."

"If you don't leave, he'll kill you."

Much to the consternation of the other diner patrons, I removed the sutures with my Swiss army knife. We left just as the waitress was about to request our exit. I bought Christine a ticket to Moses Lake with my Visa card and handed it to her as we parted. She asked for my address, so she could send my money back. I chuckled and scribbled the address on the ticket envelope. "Just send me a postcard from Moses Lake telling me you're back in school and the bruises are healing."

"I don't think they'll ever heal."

"You never know," I said as I took my fish and walked off.

I finish the story for the interviewer by telling him of a Christmas card I received from Christine. "She's back in school at Moses Lake, and she thinks she may still graduate with her class this spring. She tells me she wants to go to college and study to be a lawyer." I smile and pause at the irony. "Anyone who can lie like she can ought to be a damn good lawyer," I say.

Actually, the story ended a few days after the bus station.

The paramedics came in, all lights and sirens, with a stabbing victim. As part of the on-call surgery team, I was back in the ER. My job was to get blood from the femoral vessels and then assist another student with the Foley catheter.

There was a medic kneeling astride the patient performing chest compressions as they rolled into the trauma room. The patient had three stab wounds to the neck and upper chest. "We lost pulses three minutes out," he gasped.

"Get the chest tray open!"

"Do we have a line? Start the O negative."

"Give another milligram of epi."

I managed to get some dark blood from the groin. It became a pointless exercise. The residents had opened the left chest and were desperately trying to stop the blood loss. The attending surgeons gathered around and looked in. A sternotomy was discussed. A shunt of the lacerated carotid was attempted, but there was no blood flow. Shortly before they called it off, the chief resident grabbed my hands and stuck them inside the warm chest cavity. With his hands surrounding mine he demonstrated open cardiac compression on the lifeless heart.

It was not until the room had emptied, leaving me and another student to sew up the thoracotomy, that I noticed the houndstooth overcoat in the pile of clothes, and then the scar on her face. I heard ringing. Sweat beaded up on my brow and the walls closed in.

I was sitting outside on the stairs when the intern found me. There was a light sheen of drizzle on the pavement. "That was that girl you sewed up in the ER the other night, wasn't it?"

"Yeah."

"The cut healed up real nice."

"Yeah."

"Sometimes you have to go for the little victories."

As for the question "Why emergency medicine?" some days I'm not sure. It's just what I do.

ROBERT G. RIPLEY, M.D.
*Anchorage, Alaska*

# P A R T
# THREE

After my internship, I read Samuel Shem's book *The House of God*, about internship. One of the laws the interns were taught was "The patient is the one with the disease." I didn't yet know what that meant.

On my first night ever as a full-fledged doctor on duty, I was the only doctor in a small hospital. It was very quiet and I had plenty of time to sleep, but I stayed awake all night, terrified that I might be called Code Blue to resuscitate some patient who went into cardiac arrest. Toward dawn, I began to question why I was so scared. I wasn't going to have a cardiac arrest. I wasn't even sick. I was fine. The patient is the one with the disease. I felt reassured with that and was able to get a couple hours of sleep.

# DO YOUR BEST

It's 1984. I am a newly trained doctor. I work in a small urgent-care facility contained within a trailer twenty miles from the nearest hospital in a small suburb comprising relatively rich people who subsidize its existence. The trailer clinic has a staff of three: a young man who takes X rays, puts on splints, and cleans the floor; a young woman who is nurse, receptionist, and billing clerk; and me, the doctor. Minor medical problems are our specialty.

This evening, one of the smattering of neighborhood movie stars drops by because he is feeling skipped heartbeats. I evaluate his symptoms and check his heart rhythm. All appears normal, but we keep him on the cardiac monitor for a while.

An attractive young couple arrives, dressed for a night on the town. She is having an asthma attack. She has fear in her eyes—not a good sign. I give breathing treatments. She doesn't improve. I give intravenous drugs. She gets worse. Panic slides over her like a shadow. She can't get enough oxygen. She begins to lose consciousness. Now I'm scared. The staff is scared. Even the movie star is scared. The patient's husband is sweating, screaming, "She's dying! Do something!"

We lay her back on the gurney. She's combative, pushing us away. She's delirious, fighting. From two feet away the husband keeps screaming at me, "She's dying! Do something!" Over and over. "She's dying! Do something!" Then she stops breathing. Do something! I need to intubate her.

Intubation is a procedure requiring skill. I've done it many times. It is performed standing at the head of a patient who is lying on her back. A blade is used to push the tongue to the side while the jaw is lifted until the vocal cords are visible. Then a tube is slipped between the cords and into the trachea, allowing air to be forced into the lungs with a bag. Sounds simple, right? But often the cords are difficult to see. The patient may be gagging and thrashing, and the cords can be obscured by vomit or blood. Intubation, which can be a life-saving procedure for a patient who has stopped breathing, needs to be done right now and done right. It is used in an extreme emergency. Like this.

The woman continues thrashing. My two assistants are holding her down. The husband continues screaming at me. The blade and the tube are in my hands.

In an instant, I recall all the times during my training when I've intubated old people whose hearts have stopped and who are no longer breathing. I think of the dead and the near dead who have undergone intubation at my hands as part of that last dance of resuscitation. All the Code Blues. Full arrests. Although it seemed urgent at the time, I now realize that all those intubations were just practice for this moment. I must now do this procedure right or she will die. I also note how badly I have to pee.

I think, This is why people wet their pants when they're scared.

The screams grow distant. The room fades away. Events slow. There is just me, the blade, the tube, her throat.

I flash on an image from college. A dog caught a squirrel and crushed its chest. A bunch of us watched as the squirrel lay gasping, dying. An anguished young woman yelled at us: "Do something!" Do what? I thought. We're just kids. I am now called back to that moment. Do something! Now I'm a doctor but I still feel like a kid. I wish a grown-up would arrive and take over.

The tube slides in easily. I squirt medication directly into her lungs and ventilate her with a bag. She begins to improve. Her husband stops screaming and clutches her hand.

The movie star has been watching from his monitored bed. He is the only one without a job to do. I ask if he would please call 911, which he does. He must wonder about his own safety, having just been asked by his doctor to call 911. The ambulance arrives, and the woman and I ride to the hospital. She is much better now, awake and calm. She'll do fine.

As I drive home that night, I'm depressed. I wonder why I'm not elated. I just saved a life. I had prepared for this moment for years and tonight it all came together. I should be elated, but I am not. I am depleted. Drained. I realize why.

I never want to be that scared again as long as I live.

MARK BROWN, M.D.
*Malibu, California*

# LASTING IMPRESSIONS

It was, as Saturday afternoons go, fairly typical. Busy but in control. I barely noticed as one of the local paramedic units rolled in with a healthy-looking young man, his knee propped on a pillow, his mother close behind. Within a few minutes, one of the nurses requested that I see him because he was in quite a bit of pain. Obligingly, I went to his room. David was a handsome, athletic high school kid. In spite of his discomfort, he stoically explained that during an afternoon game of pickup basketball he felt his knee go out of joint. Indeed, he did appear to have an obvious dislocation of his patella.

I approached him with confidence and enthusiasm. After all, his problem was simple and straightforward. "We'll give you a little something for pain, and after a screening X ray of your knee, I'll just pop it right back in place," I informed him. My reassurances were met with a look of skepticism and panic. His mother, standing by the bedside, frankly and calmly informed me that she was a nurse. She asked if I would consider performing the treatment under conscious sedation, a short-acting anesthetic that would place her son in a tranquil, comfortable state during which he would be undisturbed by the minor procedure.

At this point in my career I had had limited experience with conscious sedation. As I was of petite, feminine stature, I decided that anything that would assist my finesse would be an asset and agreed to Mom's request. Following a discussion of the pros and cons, and after obtaining consent and administering a generous dose of narcotic, the nurse and I began to prepare for the procedure.

Within twenty minutes we were poised and ready. IV, monitor, and pulse oximetry were all in place. The anesthetic was given and we waited for him to settle into twilight. In about five minutes he seemed appropriately out. The nurse and I quietly moved into place. My plan was simple enough: Remove the pillows; extend the leg and simultaneously apply pressure to the lateral side of the patella. Presto— patellar reduction!

I quietly spoke some reassuring words to David as I began to lift his leg and cradle it in my arms. Suddenly his placid demeanor was replaced by moaning. Low and plaintive at first, his moans soon changed character. The tempo accelerated and the volume began to crescendo.

Criminy, I thought, I haven't even removed the pillows yet. I braced myself and continued.

"Mmmmmm. OH! Ohhhhhh! OOOOHHHHHH! OH! OH! OH!"

I felt a little flushed and looked up at his mother. "I know this all sounds quite awful, but David really can't feel much and he won't remember anything after we're finished," I assured her. She nodded quietly. Determined to get on with it, I slowly and purposefully resumed the procedure. This time my efforts were met with more animation and louder vocalizations. One could not help but notice that they were beginning to take on the distinct tone and cadence of the soundtrack from a pornographic movie. I glanced across the bed at the nurse. She had the pained expression of someone straining to maintain professional composure.

"OOOOOhhhhhh . . . OH! OOOOWWWWW! OH! OH! OH!" By now he was sitting straight up on the gurney, eyes wide open, howling wildly. "Oooooooh. Oooooow! Oh, God! Oh, God! OH! OH! OH!" As squeamish as I am about causing pain for my patients, I was becoming even more uncomfortable with the scene being created, and I was acutely aware of turning a deeper shade of red. As his bleating continued, I felt perspiration forming on my upper lip and brow. I was grateful to feel the patella suddenly settle into its proper position.

"Wh-Wh-WOW!" he shouted, then dropped back onto the pillow. For a moment he lay there quietly, eyes half closed, with a peaceful countenance. Then, slowly, he opened his eyes and met my gaze as a lazy grin spread across his face. "Got a cigarette?" he asked in a loud baritone voice.

My blush was now complete. I was sweating and my hair was tousled. I allowed an embarrassed chuckle to escape and turned to his mother. She stood with arms crossed, gazing at the ceiling, her foot tapping in nervous agitation.

Sensing her discomfort, I decided to exit. I slid open the exam room door and looked out at the nurses' station. My gaze was met by a gallery of slightly open-mouthed faces quietly staring at our room. Slowly the stares gave way to contorted smirks and grins. I glanced around the department. From nearly every exam room door there peered a curious head. I drew a deep breath and strode with pseudoconfidence to the nurses' station. "I guess they think we run a full-service department here!" the charge nurse said.

SUSAN K. SUCHA, M.D.
*Omaha, Nebraska*

# HARD TO SWALLOW

An attractive couple in dinner attire came in to the Emergency Department, both holding extremely bloody towels. The male was clutching his towel over his groin, and the woman had hers wrapped like a turban around her head. Both were very uncomfortable.

They were reluctant to talk about what had happened. Physical exam of the man revealed several deep lacerations of the penis. The woman's physical exam showed multiple puncture wounds to her scalp that were oozing blood. After some coaxing, they told their story.

They had been enjoying a candlelit dinner together and after several glasses of fine wine, they were feeling romantic. For a special dessert treat, she slipped under the table, unbuttoned his trousers, unloosed his penis, and took it into her mouth. Suddenly, in the midst of the act, she had a full-blown grand mal seizure: her jaw clamped down tightly and her head shook back and forth like a dog with a rag. In a frenzy of pain and terror, the man grabbed his dinner fork and began hacking at her head until the seizure stopped and she relaxed.

RANDAL P. DEFELICE, M.D.
*Spokane, Washington*

# PICTURE PERFECT

One Friday night the paramedics brought in an unconscious woman from a terrible car crash. We feared the worst and began searching her purse for the next of kin. While cataloging her personal items, we discovered a stack of pictures featuring the woman and a man in various revealing poses, costumes, and acts. The staff loved them and swapped them around like baseball cards. The secretary came back and said that the woman's husband was at the desk asking for information. Wanting to get these embarrassing pictures out of circulation, I gathered them together, put them in the woman's purse, and told the secretary to give it to the husband. I would be out to talk with him in a moment.

I went out to see him, expecting to recognize him on sight from his photo spread. The husband, however, was not the man in the photos.

I told him that his wife's condition was critical and that she would need to be in the intensive care unit. He listened intently, clutching the unopened purse. At this time the husband's friend came in from parking the car. I immediately recognized him from the photos.

I left them there, these two friends, and returned to care for the woman. She was admitted to the ICU and soon recovered and went home. I don't know what happened to her marriage.

As for me, I finally understood why my mom told me always to wear clean underwear.

NAME WITHHELD AT REQUEST OF AUTHOR

# GOOD FELLOW

In the great state of Texas there lives a nasty little poisonous asp called the coral snake. It has three bands of color for easy identification: red, yellow, and black. In the same area lives a copycat snake hoping to garner respect from predators by looking like the coral snake, but the copycat snake has not one whit of venom. Its bands are also red, yellow, and black, but in a different sequence. Texans, a crafty lot, have developed a little rhyme concerning these bands of color to help them distinguish the poisonous snake from the harmless one.

> Red on yellow, kill a fellow.
> Red on black, venom lack.

A man soon to be our patient, his wife, and their two children were out on a picnic. The kids discovered a multibanded snake and excitedly called the parents over. The snake was about eighteen inches long and banded alternately red, yellow, black, yellow. Mom dutifully recited her best recollection of the poem: "Red on yellow makes a good fellow!" So Dad, not in the habit of disagreeing with his wife, picked up the Texas coral snake to show his kids proper snake handling. The coral snake, although normally quite timid, was alarmed at this intrusion and chomped Dad between the thumb and forefinger. Dad screamed but had the presence of mind to drop the snake into an empty ice chest and bring it with him to the emergency room.

Dad did well with only a swollen and painful hand to show for his trust. Mom seemed a bit sheepish and the kids were alert but quiet. The emergency room staff was thrilled to have a visit from Mr. Snake and put him on show-and-tell in a plastic canister for the day before releasing him to the care of the forest service.

> Red on yellow can take a life
> Despite a well-intentioned wife.

BILL DAVIS, R.N.
*Austin, Texas*

# PLEASE TAKE A NUMBER

I t was our usual busy summer Saturday evening in the Emergency Department. Accident victims, strapped down to backboards with neck collars in place, lined the halls. A young male accident victim was being comforted by a fiftyish woman who spoke soothingly to him as she stroked his cheek and kissed his forehead. The young man looked rather anxious but lay quietly immobilized.

Before long the woman began complaining about the wait for attention. A nurse patiently explained that we were very busy, and that although it is frustrating and uncomfortable to wait, they could safely do so until a physician was available. The woman seemed not to fully understand this explanation, and went on to complain more and more loudly and less and less coherently. Finally, she announced that it was not the young man she wanted treated, it was she herself. Indeed, she did not even know the young man she was stroking, but was a registered patient herself wanting to see a psychiatrist. With one final shriek, she dramatically left the Emergency

Department, climbed into an empty ambulance, and sped off into the night.

After reporting the incident to the police, we contacted the ambulance company to inform them of what had transpired. There was a tired acknowledgment in the dispatcher's voice when he said, "I guess that explains it. Some lady just called me and said that our ambulance had pulled up on her lawn and our attendant was at her door demanding food."

STEPHEN J. PLAYE, M.D.
*Springfield, Massachusetts*

# THE DOLL HOUSE

The flaccid body of eighty-seven-year-old Frank Jenkins is rapidly wheeled past the front desk into trauma room 1. He is intubated. CPR is in progress. The paramedics have been working on him for ten minutes. He's not responding. The room is suddenly enveloped in the controlled confusion of a Code Blue, then all falls silent when the patient dies moments later. The code team disperses, leaving only the tech to clean the body and straighten the room in anticipation of family viewing.

Frank's story emerges. With winks and grins the paramedics describe the 911 call to the Doll House, one of the mobile trailers on the edge of town. They relate finding an attractive, nude young woman performing CPR. The policeman interjects that by the time he arrived at the scene for his interview, she was wearing pants but was still topless. The woman reports that Frank was a regular patron of the Doll House, and that everyone there was fond of him.

I am asked to return to trauma room 1. A spirited discussion is raging among several female staff members as to whether the erect eight-inch penis is indeed Frank's original equipment. I assess the situation and assure them Frank has benefited from the skill of a surgeon.

We need to notify the family. We finally find a number for his son and tell him his father has died.

Minutes later he is at the front desk asking to see me. We go to the quiet room and I tell him the whole story. He is profoundly disturbed and begins to piece together the explanation for behavior that has previously been a mystery. Now it all seems clear: the sudden disappearance of life savings, which must have been used to finance the prosthesis; the regular requests for extra money to pay the household bills, which must have been passed on to the Doll House.

Our eyes meet. "You know, you think you know a man, and come to find out you really don't," he says. He gazes off for a moment at nothing. Then he suddenly smiles. "But I'll bet that crafty son of a bitch died with a smile on his face."

M. C. CULBERTSON III, M.D.
*Dallas, Texas*

# LAST RITES

The little boy was four years old, with golden hair and deep blue eyes and the sweetest round face, frozen in the smile of an angel. He was also dead. Not technically, for the moment at least, but as good as, for he had drowned in a warm-water pool, and had been revived too late to save anything but a few terminal hours of heartbeats. Even that was tenuous, and it was getting harder and harder to keep him "alive" at all. What with the hopeless prognosis for his brain, and the inevitability of his early death, it was time to decide to stop.

His parents were in the ER, overwhelmed with grief, uncomprehending, frightened, guilty—like many parents I've had the great and terrible fortune to meet in moments like that. They had a special request, though: They would let us stop resuscitating the boy, on the condition that they be allowed to perform a religious ceremony, at his bedside, before he died. In fact, they had their family preacher with them.

I had no problem with this, and at eleven in the

morning, with the ER otherwise pretty quiet, I decided to stay in the room. Besides, I had agreed to do everything possible to keep his heart beating until the ceremony was complete, so one of us doctors would have to stay with him anyway.

The purpose of the ritual, I suppose, was to let the parents say good-bye to their child, in their own way. So the preacher, who went first, spoke for only a minute, and said nothing beyond the usual "all for the best" and "God's will." Then it was the father's turn; the mother wouldn't have a turn, because it wasn't a woman's role in their religion, I guess. But she stood at the head of the bed, and held her son's hand. From time to time a moan escaped her, only to be stifled as soon as she could regain control.

The father, meanwhile, stood at the other side of the child's head, and spoke to this beautiful little boy, almost as if he were really in the room with us, almost as if the ET that passed down his throat and between his vocal cords would have let him answer if his brain weren't so very dead.

"Adam, my son," he said, "you have been called to God. I know how frightened you must be, thinking that we have left you. But don't be afraid, my son, please don't be frightened. We didn't want to leave you. It's just that God took you away from us. Please don't be frightened," he repeated, perhaps to himself as much as to his child. After a pause he slowly continued. "And even though your mother and I are crying, deep in our hearts we are happy, for you."

It wasn't easy for him to say this, and he had to stop several times while trying; the mother, in her turn, could barely keep upright. "We know that you are already by God's side, because you were so dear to Him that He couldn't even wait until you were grown up to take you to Himself. Maybe we would have wanted to have you a little longer with us," he said, and though he kept from bursting into moans, his voice trailed off into silence.

It must have taken him fifteen minutes to say this, several times in slightly different ways, because his voice kept breaking down, and he had to keep struggling to regain control. The mother's sobs were more and more frequent as the ceremony went on, and at one point she threw her face against her boy's. The minister reached for her, but the father got there first, and he lifted her head, softly, and stroked her hair. He didn't say anything, and then she said, "I'll be OK," and managed after a little bit to lessen the shaking of her body, and quiet the moans from her mouth, so that gradually the father looked back at his son, and once more tried to go on. From an angle behind the mother I could see the nonrhythmic spasms of her shoulders, punctuated from time to time by a larger involuntary movement of her entire torso, and I could hear her occasional half-stifled cries.

I have watched death come many times, and seen many people struggle with it. Usually I can maintain some detachment, even when it's a sudden death, or a child's. And I am always more interested in the living, anyway, than the dead. Standing there I really didn't think about this child, or feel for his life cut short; all I could see were these two parents, with their beautiful little child lost to them, and their world shattered.

And as I watched them go through this ritual cleansing, designed to give them strength for a future that by all statistical likelihood would be full of fearsome depression, recriminations, and anger, and perhaps the end of whatever was left of their family, I kept telling myself, This is good, what they're doing, because it will enable them to go on. They need this belief, and this rationalization. And it hurts no one.

But that wasn't what I was feeling. I think I was even angrier at them than I get at the drunk drivers, or the kids who spin out on their motorcycles and die because they were too vain to wear a helmet. Certainly I have never before or since found it so difficult to remain silent, to hold in my own despair. "Stop this insanity," I wanted to yell. "There is no reason and no justification for your child to have died. None whatever. Or for sickle-cell pain, or AIDS, or even an old smoker suffocating in his own sputum. There is nothing good about any of this.

"Why are you holding back your tears, and your fury?" I went on, screaming at them inside my brain. "Your little boy is dead! No god would have stolen him, nor will any give him back. This is the world we live in, and even an eternity of heaven, if it really existed, couldn't atone for this suffering."

I didn't say anything, of course. And I really hope they found some solace. I didn't.

JEROME R. HOFFMAN, M.D.
*Los Angeles, California*

# A BLOODY MESS

It had been a slow night—the usual mix of minor trauma and accidents but nothing to get the blood really pumping. Suddenly, the EMS radio went off: "Twentyish white male with stab wound to the left anterior chest. Blood pressure eighty palpable. Pulse one forty. ETA seven minutes. We're IV positive with Ringer's wide open."

The mood in the room changed instantly. Nurses began preparing for the arrival of the patient. The trauma team arrived just as the ambulance was pulling up to the dock. When I looked at the unconscious young man, I realized he was probably about my age. I had never seen so much blood—a scarlet trail leading from the ambulance's back door all the way to the gurney he was placed on.

My job as a beginning fourth-year medical student was basically to stay out of the way and not do anything to disturb the people who knew what they were doing, so I stayed in the background and observed.

The trauma surgeon immediately took charge. He made it clear that the heart or aorta had most likely been penetrated, and in addition to needing a lot of blood, the patient's chest had to be opened.

As preparations were being made, one of the nurses spoke up: "This patient can't be given any blood. He's a Jehovah's Witness. It's right here in his wallet." She held up a card.

Things came almost to a standstill. The noisy trauma room became silent. The trauma team surgeon either did not hear the nurse or (more likely) ignored her. "Let's get that O-negative blood up here stat," he barked.

The nurse stood her ground. "I said he doesn't want any blood. I'm a Jehovah's Witness too. You know our belief about blood transfusions. I won't let you give that patient blood!"

The surgeon and nurse were now face to face. She wouldn't back down. I'd never seen anything like it. "If this guy doesn't get any blood, he'll certainly die no matter what we do," he said, raising his voice. "You know every second counts."

She looked back at the rest of us, then back to him. "If you give him the blood, he would rather be dead. He signed this card. You have to honor his wish."

No blood had arrived yet anyway, so the surgeon turned to opening the young man's chest, hoping to stop further blood loss.

As the patient's chest was opened, blood was everywhere: on the floor in puddles, on the walls, even on the ceiling. The young man's injuries were so extensive that he died before we could get a transfusion near him. In some small way, I thought to myself, the nurse had won.

The irony came later in the evening, when the police arrived. The young stab wound victim was not

a Jehovah's Witness at all. He was a thief. He had
stolen the wallet.

LAWRENCE M. LINETT, M.D.
*Loudonville, New York*

# IN SEARCH OF THE GOLDEN FALLS COBRA

I was a paramedic student at the time, doing a rotation in the Emergency Department to pick up some procedural skills. That gave me the chance to observe this case almost in its entirety without the distractions of any real duties.

It started when I was coming to work. I had parked across from the ambulance entrance to the ER and was walking across the large parking lot when a police car, siren screaming, came full throttle down the street and pulled into the Emergency entrance. The car was traveling so fast as it came up the driveway that all four wheels left the ground and sparks flew as it landed. The officer grabbed something from the trunk and ran in the entrance. His degree of urgency was unusual enough to make me wonder what was happening. When the scene was repeated less than a minute later by another patrol car, I knew something out of the ordinary had occurred. But what? An officer wounded? A hostage situation? A riot? As these possibilities crossed my mind, I hurried in to see what was causing so much action.

Entering the ER, I found a large group gathering around the officers' cargoes. In a stainless steel basin lay the head and the first twelve to fifteen inches of a large snake. The second policeman had brought the remaining five or six feet of the reptile's body and tail. Though there were seven bullet holes in the carcass, the severed head would flare and rise threateningly, poised to strike whenever anyone came too close. The snake had bitten its owner, who now lay in one of the trauma rooms.

As the paramedics were evacuating the patient from the scene, they had asked the police to kill the snake and bring it to the hospital so the ER staff could identify it and determine how to treat the victim. The police shot it in the owner's kitchen. I've often tried to imagine that scene. Were the police frightened, or were they cool and professional? How many rounds did it take to hit a writhing snake seven times? What did the kitchen look like afterward?

When I looked into the trauma room, the patient appeared pale and frightened but calm. The paramedics had treated him with a rubber tourniquet applied above the bite and a nasal cannula for oxygen. IV solution was dripping into the other arm. Nurses were checking his vital signs while curious residents and medical students were gathered three deep around the bed. I found a spot in the trauma room and remained, reviewing the action throughout his stay. This scene was too good to miss.

The patient had said the snake was a Golden Falls cobra; the problem was that nobody in this western urban hospital had any idea how to treat a cobra bite victim. The pharmacy didn't even stock rattlesnake antivenin. Police had been dispatched to at least two

suburban hospitals to obtain the antivenin )
case it might be useful. Meanwhile, the emerge.
docs tried to dig up the information needed to trea.
this unusual injury. Calls were placed to snakebite
treatment centers in India, Africa, and South America. No expert could be found who had ever heard
of a Golden Falls cobra.

While the search went on, the medical students
hustled off to the ER's small library to read about
snakebites. Every few minutes one would return and
ask the patient if he had some symptom or other.
Consistently, the patient would initially deny having
the symptom and then moments later develop it. After being asked, he reported developing tingling lips,
shortness of breath, and even double vision.

Despite the symptoms, the patient remained stable. Though his arm was becoming purple and con-
gested, no one was ready to remove the tourniquet.
At last there was a breakthrough. The police dispatcher called to let us know that his officers were
bringing in a snake expert from the local zoo. If he
could identify the snake, then maybe the doctors
could find out how to treat the injury.

The expert arrived at last, appearing somewhat
shaken after his Code 3 ride in the patrol car. After
taking a few moments to examine the remains of the
snake, he rose to face the expectant crowd. In a calm
voice he announced, "This is a Golden *False* cobra."
He went on to explain that the unfortunate animal
was only minimally venomous, and that his bite was
so unlikely to cause any harm that no treatment was
necessary.

All the tension went out of the place like air out
of a balloon. The tourniquet and IV were removed.
The patient was given a tetanus vaccination and discharged. The physicians and nurses returned to the
more usual calamities of an urban ER, and the police

took charge. The city had an ordinance outlawing exotic pets. Though the snake had been purchased in the suburbs, when the patient had brought it inside the city limits he had broken the law. No longer a victim in need of dramatic emergency assistance, he was now just another small-time criminal. A citation was issued, and the police left.

Finally, only the two of us remained. The patient sat on the gurney, the purple hue slowly fading from his forearm, the policeman's ticket in his other hand, a dazed look on his face. I wondered what he was thinking. Was he angry that the pet shop had sold him something less than he thought he'd paid for? Relieved that he was safe? Sad about losing his pet? Perhaps he was adding up his financial losses: the snake, the fine, the hospital, the ambulance, the repairs to his kitchen. Maybe he was just trying to solve the problem of getting home. The last time I saw him he was headed for the hospital lobby in search of a pay phone. He'd had his Warholian fifteen minutes of fame, and a little more, but he didn't seem to have enjoyed it much.

PAUL L. SNODDERLY, M.D.
*Fort Collins, Colorado*

# THE FIRES OF HELL

"Doc," the nurse told me, "the paramedics are coming in. They have a fifty-eight-year-old seizure patient. The paramedics know him. His seizures are fairly frequent. He's still confused, but has good vital signs and no obvious trauma. ETA is seven minutes."

The patient's name was Carl Long. He arrived groggy and not very communicative. He'd had a grand mal seizure at work. His frequent episodes had always been full-blown epileptic events that appeared to be violent, occurred without warning, and were poorly managed by medication. They were followed by the classic period of coma gradually transformed to lethargy, confusion, and, finally, understanding.

The passage from preseizure to the postseizure confusion was a Rip Van Winkle nightmare for Carl. He would be going about his business, then would awaken with crowds all around, on the ground alone, or in the confines of an emergency room. He would have no memory of the events in-between.

The last thing that Carl remembered today was being at work in the mall arcade. Years of poorly controlled seizures had limited what he could do for a living. Carl had lost many jobs when bosses, afraid of his frequent seizures, had fired him. Carl really didn't have much education. What little he possessed had been picked up here and there. He had also learned how to keep alive in a cruel, unforgiving world. At the mall, Carl got along with the kids fairly well, kept the peace in the arcade, and counseled and helped when he could. He seemed to ignore the teenage jibes of "The Dancin' Man" given to him by some.

Now, as Carl was awakening from the fog, his mind told him not to panic. He had been here many times. I began to examine him to see what, if anything, was to be done. I requested blood tests to check medication levels. Pulling aside the gown to listen to Carl's heart, I saw the waxy smooth, rippled scars of an old third-degree burn. They extended from the base of Carl's neck, down the front of his chest wall, across his shoulders, and down onto his abdomen.

"How did you get those scars? House fire?" I asked.

"No, Doc, I got lit on fire."

"What do you mean 'lit on fire'? Were you drunk or something? Or accidentally splashed with gasoline?"

"Nope. Happened when I was a boy."

"Fireworks?"

"No, Doc. I was set on fire." Carl began his story:

"When I was a boy, people like me with fits got sent to state hospitals for the insane. They'd keep us there because no one knew what to do with us. My poor parents were shamed into sending me. I remember my mom and dad fighting before I got sent away. The schools wouldn't take me. They didn't have to back then. A lot of good Christian people figured my parents must have done something evil and I was God's punishment on them. The more up-standing, nonsuperstitious ones just figured I was a genetic misfit, kind of like a badly bred animal. Hell, back then some of them even thought I should be castrated so my bad genes couldn't be passed on.

"My mom, she tried to protect me. She'd take me out like a normal kid, dress me good and all that, but I'd have these fits. I'd just fall down jerking in stores, in church, you name it. Then everyone would stand around looking scared and uncomfortable and Mom would hear all these things—she'd hear them even if they weren't said—about what a fool she was not to put me away, what a monster I was, and al-ways the questions about what was wrong with me and why did I act like that. My dad didn't under-stand any better than anyone else back then. He kept hoping I'd grow out of it. He even tried beating it out of me on occasion. When that didn't work, he started giving up on me.

"I had two brothers at home. Mom could see Dad getting more and more desperate and depressed. She'd try to cheer him up. She was a tough woman. She'd cajole and smile and try to keep going, but it finally just wore her down. I guess she figured that she had to raise the two who were normal and give up on me, even though it broke her heart. That woman really loved me. So she did what all the oth-ers did back then: She sent me to the state hospital for the mentally ill.

"It was a hell of a place, Doc! They had wards of loonies, and kids with birth defects like you couldn't believe! They had those kids with water on the brain, poor bastards. A lot of them were smart but they just had to lie there all the time because their necks wouldn't hold up their heads. 'Course, they got surgery for that now, but they didn't back then. They had kids who screamed and ripped at themselves, and kids who just stared into the walls all day. A lot of them weren't able to control their body functions, so the place smelled to high heaven, especially when it'd get hot. Some of us weren't too bad off. We'd have our seizures, but the rest of the time we'd be like the cock-o'-the-walks. It was a hell of a place, but it was what I had and I was a kid, so I played."

"How did you get burned?"

"Well, I didn't have much, of course. My parents were sent a letter about me every now and then, telling them how many seizures I was having, kind of like a batting average, I guess. Back then you didn't travel easily like you can today, so I never saw them. My mom did send me letters. Once every month I'd get something from her with a little news and a lot of love between the lines. I kept them in a shoe box under my bed, and when I felt like crying, I'd read them. You see, I couldn't run and cry to my mom. She wasn't there, but the letters were.

"One day they decided to fumigate the place, kind of like spring cleaning. They went through everybody's stuff, throwing away what they thought was junk. They figured a box of old letters wouldn't mean anything to a kid with a brain defect, so they threw them all away. Didn't ask or anything, just burned them all. Well, we got back into our ward that afternoon and it smelled of disinfectant. The walls had been washed, the windows were cracked open, the sheets were clean and stiff, the beds were all made. It looked better than it ever had, but it sure felt unfriendly. I think it bothered all of us. It was like someone coming into your house and rearranging all the furniture.

"I felt so lonely, I went to read my letters from home. They were gone. I started shrieking and crying. I was beside myself. I caused so much uproar that soon the whole ward was screaming along with me. The orderlies pretty much ran the place. Usually I was easy to get along with, so they'd let me alone. But if you got out of line, or hassled them, they'd beat you up, put you in a padded cell for days, or tie you to your bed. They figured they'd have to get me out of there.

"Two of them came in with a straightjacket for me, but I was so crazy I didn't care. I wanted someone to hit me to take away the pain I was having inside. I wanted to be knocked out or something. I was so alone, so very alone. I kicked one in the face, broke his nose, before they got me tied up. Really pissed them off. They beat on me a bit, but I still was mad, so they figured they'd *make* me shut up. They poured rubbing alcohol all over me. I guess they thought the sting and smell would knock me down, but it didn't. They beat on me some more, but I still wouldn't quiet down, so they took me into one of them padded cells. They were getting desperate. Here was a guy who never hassled them totally out of control, and nothing they did would make me slow down.

"Finally one of them, a mean son of a bitch, yelled, 'If you're going to act like the devil, you'd better remember what the fires of hell are like,' and doused me with more alcohol. I just kept spitting away and fighting, so he said, 'You just bought hell on earth, bastard!' and lit me on fire. Now I started screaming in physical pain. A couple of them started arguing about putting me out or letting me burn. While they were arguing, a nurse came by. She'd smelled all the alcohol and heard the screams. She'd figured maybe the boys were having a drunken party. Anyway, she hollered and they sprayed me down with water. They took me off to a real hospital. What you see is left over from that."

I felt like crying. I felt my impotence. "I'm terribly sorry, Carl."

"Look, Doc, it's something that happened. It caused a big stir at the time. It was a big scandal and it led to changing some of the ways they did things back then. It got me to a real hospital where they tried some new stuff on me and slowed down my seizures a whole lot. Doc, it was like that back then, but I can't live back then all my life or I'd probably kill someone." A shrug and a lopsided smile. "Probably myself. I can't change what happened. Can I get dressed now and get out of here?"

I assented, reviewed Carl's labs and noted he'd gone off his antiseizure meds again, as he often did before having a seizure. As I counseled Carl that sooner or later it might kill him, my words sounded hollow compared to the story I'd just heard.

Carl listened to my sermonette on medication, rose, and grasped my hand with his two burn-scarred hands. "Doc, thanks for listening. I know you're young and don't understand the way it was. You also don't understand this: Whether you like it or not, no matter how painful or upsetting my life may seem to you, it is my life, my pain, and my road to travel. You have your own life, Doc. You will have your own pains to bear. You worry about your pains, and I'll be praying for you. I've got my story, and, good or bad, I've learned it's mine. Thank you for your good care, and now, if you're through with me, I'll be going."

I never saw him again.

NICHOLAS M. TIMM, M.D.
*New Carlisle, Indiana*

# P A R T
# FOUR

A forty-year-old well-educated businessman appeared in the Emergency Department at 4 A.M. He was embarrassed. He reported that he and his wife had been fooling around with a large cucumber and had tried sticking it up his butt. They went too far. The cucumber slipped into the rectum and the anal sphincter slammed shut, trapping it up inside him. So here he was, after many unsuccessful attempts and with filth under his fingernails from trying to snare the vegetable from its hiding place.

He was reassured, given KY jelly and pain pills, and sent home to try and poop it out. Tired and slightly stooped, discharge instructions in hand, he walked by himself slowly down the hall toward the exit. One of our coffee-jacked, quick-witted veteran night nurses called after him: "Come on back this afternoon. We're having a butt-luck supper."

Whether used as a shield for the self or as an outlet for personal pain and fear, humor is a key ingredient in the formula for sanity after years in the Pit.

*When people behave in a nutty fashion and it
doesn't work out, they often end up in the Emergency Department. And although they can be cared
for with respect and compassion, they serve as the
fodder for an ancient pastime of the Pit: making fun
of the patient.*

# JEEPERS, CREEPERS

After discharging the last patient in the ER, I started for the sleep room at about 2 A.M. The nurse told me a moderately intoxicated man was coming in with a stuck contact lens. She offered to take it out with a suction lens remover and have me sign the chart in the morning. Half an hour later the ringing phone at the bedside told me she had not succeeded.

Examination of the patient's bloodshot eyes produced an immediate explanation: Neither eye had a contact lens in it. The patient had tried unsuccessfully to remove his cornea with his fingernails, and the nurse had failed to improve the situation with the suction cup.

Unpersuaded by the facts, the patient repeatedly grasped his cornea between his thumb and middle fingernails and pulled until his grip slipped off the tented membrane. Each attempt produced the same exclamation, "Goddamn, that hurts. See, I can get it out to here but it always pops back."

Finally, I asked to see his contact lens case. I

showed him the lenses in his case and asked,
"Whose lenses are these?" Only then did he reluc-
tantly admit he must have taken them out and for-
gotten.

Two Tylenol No. 3's got him through the night. A
follow-up exam the next day revealed normal vision,
healing corneal abrasions, a large subconjunctival
hemorrhage, and an ugly hangover.

PETER M. MIDGLEY, M.D.
*Loudersport, Pennsylvania*

# DAMSEL IN DISTRESS

In the privacy of their own home, a young couple were acting out a fantasy. She, the damsel in distress, was tied nude on the bed, spread-eagled and blindfolded. He, dressed only in mask and cape, was the superhero attempting to rescue his fair maiden. The hero climbed atop a dresser so he could "fly" to the bed and save his lover. He miscalculated his flight, struck the footboard, split his head open, and fell to the floor unconscious and bleeding. Our defenseless damsel yelled for help until neighbors investigated, only to find the house locked. They called firefighters, who kicked down the door and, with the neighbors following behind, rushed up the stairs to the bedroom.

The firemen freed the damsel and brought her superhero to the Emergency Department in his mask and cape. Despite the red faces, all did well.

BRENDA HILL, R.N.
*Syracuse, New York*

# LAUNDER YOUR MONEY

A thirty-six-year-old man was brought to the ER following a forty-eight-hour cocaine binge. After repeated seizures, he was unconscious and had a temperature of 104 degrees. We started IVs, monitored his heart, stopped his seizures, and placed him in a wooden cooling tub in an effort to get his temperature down. I had to place a catheter through his penis and into his bladder to monitor his urine output. As I pulled back his foreskin, a tightly folded twenty-dollar bill popped out. We laughed, and joked about never knowing where your money has been. I put it in the safe with his clothes. He was still in the ER when he finally regained consciousness. Now indignant that he had been brought to the hospital in the middle of his party, he demanded to leave. As I returned his belongings, I told him how I had found the twenty dollars in his foreskin and locked it up for him. His grateful reply: "It was a fifty, bitch!" In his dreams.

DENISE ABADIE, R.N.
*Metairie, Louisiana*

# UNSAFE SEX

O ne day when examining a rape victim, I found pieces of napkin bearing a chicken restaurant logo protruding from her vagina. Later that same day we received a man with a gunshot wound to his leg. While preparing him for surgery, I pulled back his foreskin to insert a catheter and found shreds of napkin with the same restaurant logo. The police were notified and he was promptly arrested.

DENISE ABADIE, R.N.
*Metairie, Louisiana*

# THE HUMAN VINEYARD

An elderly female comes to the Emergency Department complaining: "I got the green vines in my virginny."

The patient reports a two-week history of a vine growing from her vagina. On physical examination it is discovered that she does indeed have a vine growing out of her vagina, about six inches in length.

A pelvic exam reveals a mass which is easily removed from the vaginal vault, vine still attached. Upon extraction, the patient reports that her uterus had been falling out and that she "put a potato in there to hold it up" and subsequently forgot about it.

JOHN RIORDAN, M.D.
*Charlotte, North Carolina*

# HARD COPY

The gentleman looked quite uncomfortable as he slowly shuffled past us, following the triage nurse to his room. When the nurse returned and wrote down the pertinent information on the board, the nurses began to giggle. The chief complaint was "Penile laceration."

Upon entering the room, I found a middle-aged man sitting with his legs over the side of the gurney, his groin covered by a sheet, shaking his head to himself. I introduced myself and asked him what happened. His reply went something like this:

"I am so embarrassed, Doc. You see, my boss has been riding my back for the longest time and I just decided I'd had enough. I decided to quit, but I wanted to show him how I really felt about him. So at five o'clock, when everyone had left for the day, I turned the copier back on and made a copy of my hand flipping the bird. I wrote a note at the bottom telling my boss to screw himself, and put it right in the middle of his desk. Then I decided that wasn't good enough. I went back to the copier, checked

**99**

again to make certain I was alone, dropped my
pants, lifted up the cover, and put my manhood on
the machine. But when I pushed the button to make
the copy, the cover fell down!''

The patient suffered only minor abrasions and
contusions, fortunately. I never found out if he had
the machine set for enlargements.

NAME WITHHELD AT REQUEST OF AUTHOR

# SHORT TAKES I

---

Back in the days when IUDs were more common, I had a woman come in asking to have a DC-7 inserted. Another woman told me she used condominiums for birth control.

People come in to the ER for all sorts of strange reasons. I'm sure that my most nonemergent chief complaint will never be topped. A male adolescent came in at 2 A.M. with a complaint of lint in the belly button.

ER staff deal with difficult families. There was a man who insisted that his mother-in-law be admitted to the hospital so that he could go on a fishing trip. He had his fishing gear on and was obnoxious. The mother-in-law was also obnoxious . . . but not sick.

Two psychiatric patients had met in our hospital and married. They came in one night insisting that they had been sexually assaulted by aliens and requested an examination.

\*   \*   \*

A fifty-year-old woman came in to the ER with multiple problems, most of which were very difficult to solve. She had recently divorced her husband and married her twenty-year-old stepson. Her new husband sucked his thumb and was very weird. The more I inquired about the lady's problems, the more bizarre the story became. I finally asked the lady what I could do to help her. Her answer: "Just sing me some country music."

SYLVIA SYDOW, M.D.
*Denver, Colorado*

# CONSTIPATION

One evening a middle-aged man was brought in via ambulance with severe abdominal pain. He related a history of constipation unrelieved by Fleet enemas or laxatives. Frustrated, he gave himself an enema of his own special concoction—Drano! He went directly to surgery. The surgeons later told me that his entire colon was "charcoaled." He lived for about two weeks before dying of overwhelming abdominal infection.

DAVID VILABRERA, M.D.
*Holliswood, New York*

# DOCTOR KNOWS BEST

An adolescent female came to the Emergency Department with a complaint of lower abdominal pain. The emergency physician took a thorough history and did a complete physical examination, including a pelvic exam. All this was normal. Although the patient denied any sexual activity, the physician had been surprised before, so he sent off a serum pregnancy test. The test came back positive. The physician returned to the young woman's room.

DOCTOR: "The results of your pregnancy test came back positive. Are you sure you're not sexually active?"

PATIENT: "Sexually active? No, sir, I just lay there."

DOCTOR: "I see. Well, do you know who the father is?"

PATIENT: "No. Who?"

SCOTT OSLUND, M.D.
*Sunnyvale, California*

# THE GRAPES OF WRATH

A young woman signed in complaining of a purple discharge. I had heard of green, yellow, pink, and other assorted shades, but purple? She was taken back to one of the OB/GYN exam rooms, and the pertinent questions were asked: Are you pregnant? When was your last period? How many times have you been pregnant? And so on. One question drew an interesting response.

"Are you using any type of birth control?" she was asked.

"Yes," she responded, "a diaphragm." I was delighted. It seemed so few of our patients did use contraceptives.

"But I've only been using it a few days," she added. I nodded.

"So tell me about the purple discharge," I continued.

"Ain't much to tell. I got the prescription filled for the diaphragm that the doctor gave me and the discharge started almost right away. I thought maybe I was allergic to it or something."

"So the discharge started almost as soon as you began using the diaphragm," I reiterated. She nodded affirmatively. "And you're using the spermicide jelly with it?" I asked.

"Look. The doctor told me to use the diaphragm and the jelly with it, and I did," she said.

I nodded understanding, then had a sudden flash of insight.

"What kind of jelly are you using in the diaphragm?"

"I don't remember—I think it was grape."

BARBARA NUTINI, R.N.
*Independence, Kentucky*

# THE LONG WAY HOME

A ninety-two-year-old woman suffered a full cardiac arrest at home and her family called for an ambulance. The ambulance transported the patient with CPR in progress.

She arrived in our ER and, after thirty minutes, we were unable to resuscitate her. I pronounced her dead and went out to tell her seventy-eight-year-old daughter.

I looked at her gently and said, "I'm sorry, ma'am, but your mother didn't make it."

Shocked, she looked at me and shouted, "Didn't make it? Where could they be? She left in the ambulance forty-five minutes ago!"

GEORGE R. DREW, D.O.
*Rockford, Michigan*

# COLOSTOMY

A thirty-five-year-old female came to my Emergency Department with a complaint of mild abdominal pain. The patient had a colostomy from surgery for a previous gunshot wound to the abdomen. While reviewing her social and employment histories, I saw that the patient had stated, "I work the street." I asked her to clarify what she meant. She replied, "I get money for having sex—twenty-five dollars for a guy to do me [points to her vagina] and ten dollars for a guy to do it [points to her colostomy]."

RICHARD A. OYLER, M.D.
*Mobile, Alabama*

# YESTERDAY

One spring day while at work in the Emergency Department, we received word on the radio of a big-rig accident with serious injuries to the driver. The patient was brought into the department barely alive, and after an hour of attempted resuscitation was pronounced dead. The staff involved dispersed to their other duties, the body was taken to the morgue, and the cleanup crew arrived to restore the trauma room. Exhausted, I went to the physicians' dictation area to complete the chart and notify the next of kin.

While sitting there, I heard a distorted, metallic-sounding melody coming from the direction of our clerk, seated behind me. It repeated over and over until I finally had to turn and ask, "Pat, what is that sound?" She held up a manila envelope containing the deceased's personal belongings. She looked at me oddly, pointing to the envelope. A tune was coming from inside. She answered, "It's his watch."

She opened the envelope and produced a small novelty watch, capable of playing a selection of three or four tunes. Though the watch was smashed, it repeatedly chimed the old Beatles tune, "Yesterday ... all my troubles seemed so far away...."

MICHAEL M. KNOTT, M.D.
*Tahoe City, California*

# THE SPECIMEN

A newly arrived Mexican immigrant, knowing not a word of English, arrived in the ER indicating pain in his abdomen. He was a handsome and macho young man, with a tight T-shirt to show off his well-muscled body. We tried to develop the young man's story through pointing and gestures. A physical exam showed some low abdominal tenderness. I wanted some lab tests. I pointed to his forearm for a blood test that I would order, and I pointed to his groin for a urine test. I handed him a small plastic bottle and led him to the toilet to produce a urine specimen. After ten minutes, he still had not emerged from the bathroom. One of the nurses needed the bathroom so she knocked on the door. After some rustling, the young man appeared, flushed and sweating, but beaming proudly. He handed the nurse his specimen container. It was filled with semen.

B. TOMKIW, JR., M.D.
*Fair Oaks, California*

# DO NO HARM

The man had suffered chest pains for days but had resisted his wife's urging that he seek help. Finally, she drove him to the ambulatory ER entrance. At the curb, we recommended a stretcher, and, when he refused that, a wheelchair. But he was cranky and insisted on walking. At the door he collapsed, unconscious. One of our physicians countershocked the patient, brought him back to life, and quickly stabilized and transferred him to the cardiac unit. Out of the hospital in two weeks, the man sued the ER and the physician because he had broken his nose and cut his lip in the fall.

HUGH F. HILL III, M.D.
*Bethesda, Maryland*

# OUT OF STEP

A young farmer caught his right leg in a farm implement, severing it above the ankle. He was brought in by ambulance in intense pain and anguish but otherwise was stable.

Meanwhile, back on the farm, the other farmhands thought it prudent to find the severed foot, which they did. It was still in its work boot, still warm. They jumped in the truck and drove off toward the hospital.

In their haste, they crashed the truck. Although no one was injured, the truck was disabled. Desperate to have the body part transported to the hospital, they flagged down the next car, which was driven by a plump woman in hair curlers and a housecoat on her way to the market. The farmers rushed up to her with the bloody stump sticking out of the top of the boot, handed it to her through the window, and pleaded for her to take it to the hospital.

I happened to be in the hallway near the door when she walked in. "Here," she said with a cigarette in one hand and the foot in the other. "Some-

one asked me to bring this foot up here." I thanked
her and took the foot up to the OR.

KIRK V. DAHL, M.D.
*Eau Claire, Wisconsin*

# PERSEVERANCE

---

A young male entered the walk-in entrance to our ER one busy Sunday afternoon shift, holding a hand over a bloodstained shirt. When the over-whelmed triage nurse didn't acknowledge him for several minutes, he calmly walked to the registration desk and informed the startled clerk that he had been shot in the chest. After the man was rushed into our trauma room, his unluckiest-ever story un-folded.

It seems that he had been depressed for several weeks, and two days earlier had decided to commit suicide. He took a bottle of Valium and a fifth of vodka and fell asleep in his bed, fully intending to never wake up again. Unfortunately, the combina-tion was not lethal, and he did wake up, albeit thirty-six hours later, with a tremendous hangover. Deciding that something else was needed to com-plete the job, he filled up the bathtub, got in, and slit both wrists with a razor blade. Alas, the bleeding was all venous and clotted off after several minutes, leaving him sitting in a pink-tinged lukewarm bath-tub.

He climbed out of the bathtub and decided to hang himself from the dining-room light fixture using his belt. The light fixture tore from the ceiling and he crashed to the floor with such force that he fell *through* the dining-room floor into the basement. Battered but not beaten, he looked around the basement for something to finish the job. He found a .22 caliber bullet but *no gun.* He decided to hold the bullet with a pair of pliers and, pressing it against his sternum, took several whacks at the compression end of it with a ball-peen hammer. On the third whack the bullet went off. He fell to the floor and looked down to see a bullet hole on the left side of his chest. After lying on the floor for twenty minutes, he decided that maybe he really did not want to die and drove himself to the ER.

Our evaluation showed that the bullet had harmlessly bounced off a rib and was lying in the subcutaneous tissue of the left chest.

JAMES DOUGHERTY, M.D.
*Akron, Ohio*

# SHORT TAKES II

A patient said: "Doc, my wife has a rat in her pussy and every time I do her, my dick hurts."

"A rat?"

"Yeah, a rat that bites me whenever I get in there."

I did a pelvic exam and found a needle in her vagina left there by the surgeon who had performed her hysterectomy. Ouch.

A thirty-year-old male in custody has swallowed a bag of cocaine. We give him charcoal and sorbitol to make him poop it out. When it comes out, he tries to grab it and hide it. The police see him and run over and try to get the bag. They start fighting over it. Charcoal, cocaine, and shit go flying everywhere. What a mess.

A thirty-five-year-old male comes in with a deformed right forearm that is swollen and extremely tender. He says he just fell off a ladder.

"Doc, this is killing me, can I get some pain meds before I get an X ray?" I say, "Sure." When I have a chance, I look at his X ray. There's a fracture, but it's at least a year old—well healed, but at an angle. I walk back from X-ray to discuss this with him and he's gone. Outsmarted by a drug addict.

A forty-year-old female came in after jumping into a tree from the third-story window of a burning house. She was obviously high on something, but she said she felt fine. She had a normal physical exam, with the exception of a nick to her left flank and a small bump on the right side of her chest. I asked her how long the bump had been there. She replied, "I ain't got no bump on my side."

Her blood pressure suddenly began to drop, so I ordered X rays. They revealed a tree branch lodged diagonally through her torso. The surgeon later told me what he had found. The branch had entered her left flank, caught her spleen, punctured her diaphragm, and was pushing on her right chest wall.

She was right. Prior to that jump, she didn't have no bump on her side.

KENNETH A. WALLACE III, M.D.
*Detroit, Michigan*

# THEFTPROOF

One night while I was working in a trauma center in Detroit, paramedics brought in a young man who had been hit in the head with a pipe. He looked dazed and smelled as though incontinent of stool. We undressed him, and our eyes confirmed what our noses had suspected. We were surprised to find a car key in the stool in his shorts. We asked him how this key had happened to find its way to such an unlikely location. He replied, "They were trying to steal my car, so I put my key down there and shit myself. That's when they hit me in the head."

Commending him on both his quick thinking and his ability to defecate at will, we agreed that without a good cup of coffee and a newspaper *we* would be pedestrians.

CHRIS PFAENDTNER, M.D.
*Janesville, Wisconsin*

# REGISTRATION

It was a busy afternoon at the Emergency Department, Saint Mary's Hospital, Knoxville, Tennessee. The department doors opened and a pretty and prim young lady walked up to the reception desk. The receptionist, as was her custom, not looking at the patient asked:

"Name"—and typed.

"Address"—and typed.

"Zip code"—and typed.

"Phone"—and typed.

"Religion"—and typed.

"Sex"—(no answer) . . .

"SEX"—(no answer) . . .

"SEX"—(pause) . . .

Finally, the young lady said, "Well, if it's any of your business—two times in Chattanooga."

A. L. JENKINS, M.D.
*Knoxville, Tennessee*

# P A R T
# FIVE

I was sent a story by a nurse, David Fox, called "Theo's Dream," in which he recalls a meeting between the ER night-shift charge nurse, Bunny Bradford, and a cocky new intern.

Bunny welcomed the morning. The night had been long and tedious, made more tedious by the presence of the new intern, Len. Early in the shift, Len had made the mistake of thinking that a nurse named Bunny must be an airhead. He held that thought only briefly before Bunny took time to remind him that she had been working in the ER when he was still raising his hand for permission to pee. Without a pause, she further informed Len that Bunny was a name chosen by her misguided parents, and that as yet, he was too new and inexperienced to do anything more complicated than ask, "How may I help you?"

Hearing their exchange, the chief resident only grinned and shook his head.

Len blushed and stared at the chart in his hand. "Fucking ER nurses," he mumbled to himself, "they think they're hot shit."

He was right.

ER nurses are the Top Guns of their profession. In few other areas do nurses practice with such autonomy and responsibility as they do in the Pit. They have a reputation for being independent, assertive, and tough.

New ER nurses think the hardest part of the job will be the rapid pace and the trauma. But those who stay soon realize that the true challenge is the human misery. It's wearing. The demands and complaints are many and the thank-you's are few. It's easy to feel used up.

So to survive, ER nurses develop a protective shield. They learn to parcel out caring when needed, but to save some for the next guy.

They also learn to save a little for themselves.

# NURSING

## Anita Jones, R.N.
## Lancaster, California

The request has come from hospital administration. The gift foundation is planning a fund-raising event for the emergency room. They need some heartwarming ER nursing stories to share at the program. Sounds easy. I've been here a long time. I've kept a journal of my experiences. I'll just flip through and pull out some good ones.

Heartwarming stories from the ER. I search. I read. I'm stunned. I can't find any.

There are scores of stories in the ER every day—heartbreaking, heart numbing, heart tickling, heart stopping—but heartwarming? Not really, not the warm fuzzy kind. It's scary. Have I become so cynical that I can't see anything warm in my work?

I read them again, seeing them as they are. I cry. I laugh. All my memories and the feelings they revive begin to warm my heart.

It feels good.

Here are some of the stories I found.

# THE SAVE

About the best feeling I have is when we get a "save." A guy walks in—obvious heart attack. Pale. Clammy. Chest pain. Looks bad.

The team kicks in. Get him in bed. Heart monitor on. Get vital signs. Start the IV, oxygen. Get a second IV. Blood for labs.

We're working on both sides of the bed when I hear a funny breath. I glance up at the patient. He's fading. Glance up at the monitor. He's in VTach.

No chance to speak, just react—*thump!* Hit him in the sternum.

Glance at the monitor. He's converted. Regular rhythm restored. Breathing goes back to normal.

We look at each other across the bed. Surprise. Relief. Success!

I look at the patient. There's confusion on his face. "Hey, are you OK? Sorry I had to hit you."

And back we go. Start the meds. Call the cardiologist. Get an EKG. This guy got here just in time! Yeah, team!

It's not always like that.

Sometimes someone comes in talking to you and then just dies. You're doing the same things. You hear the funny breath that tells you the breathing is stopping. You react, do all the right things, and he dies anyway.

It's harder then. Different than when someone comes in dead or near dead. More personal.

You always hear the same comment, "He was just talking to me!"

Maybe he was just hanging on till he got someplace where he felt safe enough to let go.

When someone comes in with resuscitation in full swing, we usually just jump in, do a job. We don't think of the person—at least not till later, when we face the family's grief.

# THREE BROTHERS

It was a week before Christmas during the coldest spell we'd had in years. Three little brothers, ages one to four, were brought in by the sheriff. They'd been alone in their unheated house for possibly five days. Their dad was in jail, and Mom was who knows where.

The oldest one, a chatty kid, said they hadn't eaten for at least two days. The baby's wet feet were white with cold. The middle brother's feet stank so bad when we took off his shoes that I felt nauseated. I wondered what their lives had been like during that cold December week. We hustled those boys into a warm bath.

A message was sent to the kitchen that we needed food for three kids who hadn't eaten in days. Usually it takes thirty to forty minutes to get a food tray from the kitchen. This time, in less than five minutes, three ladies personally delivered food to the room.

The four-year-old gobbled it down. Baby brother cuddled up with his bottle. The three-year-old just fell asleep after his bath. I called a friend with kids near their ages and asked for some hand-me-downs. She hurried right over with clean clothes for all.

Charting our treatments for them brought tears to my eyes. The treatments were so simple, something every kid deserves. Heat. Nourishment. Hygiene.

But the warm fuzzies end there. The deputy came back later in the week to tell us Mom was in jail and the brothers were placed, separately, in foster homes. They'd stuck it out for a cold lonely week but they wouldn't be together at Christmas.

# LIFE AFTER DEATH

Sometimes our duties extend beyond life.

We have just completed a Code Blue, a resuscitation attempt on a youthful senior citizen.

It was a futile effort. We knew that when we started.

She was the innocent victim of a drunk driver.

She'd been hit and dragged. The sheriff said sixty feet. Her injuries were indescribable.

Even trauma-hardened ER personnel were disturbed by the violence inflicted on her body.

Now I look at her still form and think of her husband sitting in the small waiting room reserved for grieving families. He'll probably want to see her. We usually encourage a family to see their loved one before the body is permanently altered by the neat perfection of the embalmer. It helps bring home the reality; helps start the grieving process.

But this time I'm not sure. We can cover her body, but her face . . .

Bouncing under the car has ripped her scalp open. The tissue covering her forehead has been split apart, exposing her glistening skull.

We begin to clean up the room, to clear the evidence of the struggle for life.

I leave for a few minutes to attend to some other patients. When I return, I observe a miracle in progress.

The nurse in the room has carefully cleaned this woman's head and is using clear tape to gently pull her face together. I am amazed at the difference. She has been changed from an unrecognizable form to an identifiably attractive woman. A simple towel turban to hide her wounds completes the transformation. Her elegantly manicured hand is placed casually on top of the sheet.

Now the grieving husband is able to face her. He probably will always carry the memories of this room, of this moment.

But at least in his memories he will recognize his wife.

# WHAT MIGHT HAVE BEEN

It's 7 A.M., a new shift. Not even time for coffee before the radio alarms. Auto accident. Two kids headed for home two hours away. Their truck flipped off a bridge into a wash. Now they're on a detour to the ER.

He looks worse than she does, an obvious candidate for a few days in the ICU.

She doesn't look too bad. She's awake, knows what's happening. She moves her arms and legs. She says her neck is sore.

She lies patiently, her body immobilized on a hard board, waiting for X rays.

I call her mom and dad.

How do you tell parents two hours away that their daughter's been in an accident? You want to convey calm without lying about the seriousness of the situation. And you know nobody's calm after a call from the ER.

I tell mom she looks pretty good initially, a few aches and pains but we're just getting started, no X rays yet.

Parents are on their way.

Neck X rays are completed first. The radiology report's negative, so off come the cervical restraints. I check her over again and find a couple of new aches. Back she goes to X-ray to find a fractured knee and shoulder.

Her neck is still hurting. I feel uneasy. The X rays have been checked by the doctor, she has no numbness, no tingling, no loss of movement, but I have this nagging voice mumbling deep inside.

She asks for a pillow. The nagging voice sputters. I compromise with a small folded towel behind her head. Five minutes later she tells me her hand is tingling. The voice inside me explodes with an accusation! Why didn't you listen to me!

My calm exterior remains. I slide the towel out and grab the doctor. We reimmobilize her neck.

The films go back to the radiologist with the new symptoms. Another look shows a break in her second cervical vertebrae. Nerves to her entire body pass through this bone. Nerves that control breathing, movement, feeling. Nerves that control her present and future.

Inside I am screaming. Outside I am calm.

Without the towel, the tingling is gone. Relief! Sensation and movement are normal. Whew!

Mom and Dad arrive.

I have good news and bad news. Your daughter's alive—but she has a broken neck. Your daughter's not paralyzed—but she has to wear a brace screwed into her head for the next few months.

Inside, I am drained. I'll remember this girl forever. Daily in this job I see the frailty of life. Today I am slapped in the face with it.

I wheel her to her hospital room. I stay with her while the neurosurgeon places the head screws.

She is great, very brave. She thanks me for my care. Sends me flowers. Promises to keep in touch.

That night I don't sleep well, haunted by what might have been.

# ID

He looks about fourteen or fifteen. It's hard to tell with the animation missing from his face. One thing is sure—he'll never be any older.

We know him only as John Doe. We need to find his real name. We look for a wallet, a card with a phone number—hopefully an address.

All we find are three pictures—yearbook photos of pretty girls. There's writing on the back of two: "Luv ya always" and "To Rocky, Love, Maria." It's a start at least.

There's some writing on his chest, a neat script below his right nipple. It says "Rocky." Must be him. He doesn't look like a Danielle (the name scratched on his right bicep).

The beeper on his belt is full of messages. It went off a couple of times during CPR. We didn't have time to reply just then.

One phone number appears twice. A girl answers and we take a chance: "Hello, Maria?"

"Yeah."

"Do you know a guy named Rocky who rides a motorcycle?"

"Uh-huh."

"We need to get in touch with his parents right away."

# USO

It's a crowded Saturday in the ER.

There's a steady parade of people with the usual complaints—headaches, fevers, broken bones, lacerations—interrupted by the occasional ambulance with a more serious delivery.

I glance up to see a man walk by.

Double take!

I know that face. It's the same one I see on record covers, on TV, in movies. The guitar and glitter are missing, a two-day beard is showing, but the face is unmistakable.

What's he doing here?

I find out he's with a kid. They've been out camping and the kid has hurt his arm.

We get the arm fixed up and they're ready to leave. There's a gentle ripple of excitement among the staff as they realize he's here. We're all smiling at each other, trying to be aware without infringing on his privacy.

I find myself humming one of his songs and hear someone else doing the same.

As he's leaving I see him talking with the secretary, writing things down. I hear her say my name, and look over his shoulder to see what he's writing. He says he wants to send us tickets to his concert next month—the concert that will be a sellout in one day. He takes our names and signs a couple of autographs. He lets me shoot a Polaroid. We proudly display it on a mobile we've made with ER staff pictures.

Sunday we play his songs nonstop and sing along all day.

In the ER, we often feel like soldiers in a little war zone—a lot of tension with few bright spots. We usually have to make our own laughter. He was our USO show.

# THANKSGIVING DINNER

The big family Thanksgiving dinner has been interrupted by two four-year-old cousins who got into Grandma's purse and ate her heart pills.

Now, with the turkey getting cold at home and their moms standing nearby, the two little cousins are sitting side by side on the gurney.

Big towels are draped around their necks, big basins are in their laps.

They're getting lots of attention.

Syrup of ipecac is mixing with the pills in their stomachs, getting them ready to throw up.

They're smiling. They're still happy. The ipecac tasted OK.

They're not sure just what they are waiting for. Their smiles are about to fade, but before that happens, we shoot a couple of Polaroids for the moms. Pictures to save of cousins and their big basins, so when they've grown big and know it all, they can be reminded of this Thanksgiving.

# TRAUMA

It's a freak accident.

An elderly man has fallen from his roof.

We call the surgery team. His chest has been pierced by a stick protruding from the ground. The injury is near vital organs—heart, lungs, large arteries. We call for the blood bank to stand by.

When he arrives we are pleasantly surprised. His vital signs are OK.

There appears to be no real damage to his vital organs. No broken neck. He is lucky!

But look again. His legs don't move. His arms are numb. What?

That stick. It has angled up through his chest, just missing heart, lungs, and vessels, and has severed his spinal cord.

My reaction is strange. I can't really explain it. I don't understand it. This type of injury is always tragic. It just seems worse somehow when the patient is an elderly person. To have survived all the minefields of life to come to this. Trauma happens to the young. Illness happens to the old. When the roles are reversed, everything is thrown out of balance.

# DO EVERYTHING!

It's almost time to go home.

An old lady is brought to the ER by ambulance from the nursing home.

She has a massive infection, pneumonia. Every breath is a gurgle. Her temperature is very high, oxygen level very low. She has no apparent awareness of anything. Her eyes are open, staring. Her skin is like tissue paper.

Most startling is her body.

It's stiff, locked into an immobile position—a foam wedge is tucked under her upper body, because without it her head and upper back are raised from the bed with no support.

Her legs are twisted. She has severe deformities of her arms and shoulders, large bruises there—apparent fractures of fragile joints and bones.

She appears to be on her way to death.

Call her doctor; surely she must be a "no code" patient! Let her go quietly. One compression on her fragile chest will do her in for sure. Nobody deserves such suffering.

The doctor speaks to her son by phone, explains the situation.

The son says, "Do everything!"

I'm furious!

Where is he, this son who wants everything?

Make him come here and see just what "everything" means—the tubes, the suctioning, the chest compressions, the cracking ribs, the needles, the catheters, the noise, the pain, the indignity. Who is he to demand that we assault his mother in this way! Well, he got what he asked for.

I cried all the way home in my car.

# FOUR HOURS IN TRIAGE

I'm working a twelve-hour shift. The first eight hours have been spent in the treatment area ("the back," we call it). Now it's my turn to do triage—the Pit. Time to take on the job of sorting and categorizing—immediate, urgent, delayed, totally nonurgent. The patients are trickling in: Fever (we're in the middle of flu season). Cough. Laceration. Headache. Fever—give Tylenol. Sprained ankle—give a cold pack. Cough. Prescription refill.

"My baby's having trouble breathing!" Two weeks old, color dusky blue. His chest is caving in with labored respirations.

All his energy is spent on breathing. He has none left to cry or move.

"He's been sick like this for three days."

Three days! I'm thinking this baby's going to die right here! What has this mom been doing for three days?

"Mom, you wait over there."

I grab baby and dash back to a treatment room, calling for help as I run.

We have a sick one here! Call respiratory therapy. Get an IV ready. Temperature is only ninety-four degrees. Probably a massive infection. The pediatric resuscitation team takes over. Baby's color is improving already.

I go back to talk to Mom, give her a progress report, get more information. "Was the baby OK at birth?"

"Well, there were amphetamines found in his body when he was born."

Amphetamines *found* in his body! Well, Mom, who the hell put them there?

I try to hide my feelings of disdain. I tell Mom her baby is very sick and the doctor will talk to her as soon as they get the baby stabilized.

Back I go to triage, where the line is lengthening. Laceration. Crushed finger. Fever.

"Baby in van."

The Hispanic-looking man interrupts and gestures for me to follow.

He speaks little English. I speak little Spanish.

I grab some clean towels and follow him out through the waiting-room crowd to a van parked outside the door.

I crawl inside, where his wife is lying with a small naked daughter, wet and bloody, between her legs.

Baby looks bright eyed, alert. Color is pink and healthy. Mom looks OK too. There's a normal amount of bleeding.

There is another woman in the van with her, maintaining Mom's modesty, replacing the blankets I've moved to look.

Apparently she's the acting midwife.

I run back for help. Call for a gurney. Grab warm blankets. Grab the OB delivery kit.

Crawl back inside the van. Wrap up the baby. Clamp and cut the cord.

Mom is moved onto the gurney for an anticlimactic trip to the delivery room to deliver the placenta.

Baby and I head up toward the nursery. Oops, go back to get Dad. I need him to go with me. I don't even have a name on this little one and want no chances of any mix-up! He can stay with the baby until an absolute ID is made.

What a little cutie she is, peeking out from the blanket with the bright eyes of an alert newborn! I smile going up in the elevator with the baby and Dad.

Then, hurry back to triage.

Where were we? Oh, I remember: fever, laceration, cough, vomiting, miscarriage, fever, earache, cough, leg pain . . .

"My baby's having trouble breathing." Oh, no, not again! Chest caving in, wheezing.

This baby is alert and more active than the previous one. Color is better this time. But still he is puffing away—working too hard at breathing. Back we go, to a treatment room. (I think the nurses working in the back must hate to see me coming, the bearer of another disaster.) Call respiratory therapy!

Then back to my post. The dinner-hour crowd is gathering, lining up at the door of the triage room: fever, vomiting, congestion, bladder infection. Get a urine sample.

"My son has had four seizures today. I think it's because of some medication he took. He's never had seizures before today." His temperature is 101 degrees. High enough to cause a seizure? Not usually.

The toddler is sitting on Dad's lap. He appears sick but alert, a little fussy.

Suddenly it starts, seizure number five. Eyes roll out to side; hands, then arms grow stiff, start to twitch. The whole body gradually joins in.

Check the child and question: "Dad, are you OK?

Can you hold him? Let's just carefully carry him back to the doctor." Stay calm. Don't alarm the crowd. A seizing kid always looks bad.

We lay him down on a bed. Nurses join in. Color is turning blue. Get the oxygen. Dad is anxious. Is he breathing? Call respiratory therapy. Breathing is OK. Heartbeat's OK.

The team takes over, start IVs. Give medicine to stop the convulsions.

I take Dad back to the family waiting room to find Mom and explain what's happening.

Then back to triage: splinter, lip laceration, anxiety reaction, suture removal, fever, chest pain, headache . . .

7:00 P.M. Done! Fresh troops have arrived. Time to go home! A-h-h-h-h. What a day!

# WHAT AM I DOING HERE?

There aren't many jobs like mine.
There aren't many jobs where your workday
  ends the way mine did today:
By washing the face of a 16-year-old boy.
Cleaning red crusts from his sparse chin whis-
  kers,
Straightening him up, helping him get pre-
  sentable.
And then bringing his father and sister to see
  him,
So they can see it's really true.
So they can see he's really dead.

# INTIMATE STRANGER

I'm just breaking for lunch when the radio call comes. Single-car rollover, nineteen-year-old male.

Condition serious—unconscious—head and facial trauma—over a liter of blood lost already—paramedics trying to control his airway.

He's a long way out. They've dispatched a helicopter.

This will not be an easy one. Forget lunch. Call the troops. Prep the room. Blood is hanging. We're ready.

When he arrives, it's worse than the paramedics reported. We scoop him on the gurney and run from the helicopter. We almost never run from the helicopter, but blood is pouring from his face. There is so much it is hard to recognize his features.

The docs surround him to make an airway and stop the bleeding. We pump the blood in as fast as we can while it pours out. If we win with his blood pressure, we lose with the bleeding. The score is close. It's hard to tell who's ahead and our guts say it's not us.

His head is a spongy mass, but the rest of his body looks perfect—only a couple of scratches.

We restart his heart a couple times.

As usual, we laugh some and make little jokes as we work. We don't know him. We don't want to know him right now. We don't think about him as a person. A housekeeper comes in to clear away some of the rubble. She glances at him and comments what a shame it is—he's so young. I nod in agreement but look at him and think how strange it is—the lack of human connection I feel. Right now he is trauma number RT7698 and he is dumping— testing our skills to the max.

Finally he is stable enough to survive a CT scan of his brain, or what is left of it. The CT confirms our worst suspicions. To diagnose brain death is probably only a formality.

After three exhausting hours, we get him to the ICU. It is a relief to let someone else worry about his dipping blood pressure and swollen brain.

Little details of his recent life are gradually discovered. His name is Richard and he is a freshman in college. We learn he lives out of state. I talk to his friend who will call his parents across the country.

I'm glad I don't have to tell them.

An ICU nurse pulls a card from his wallet and shows it to me. The picture shows a handsome, smiling young guy with brown hair. I stare and feel my throat tighten.

Why did she have to show me that picture! Now he is real.

I liked it better when we were strangers.

# SCREAMING

It's the middle of the afternoon.

There's been an auto accident. Ambulances have brought the injured to the ER. The gurneys are already full, but we quickly shuffle beds around to find places for the new arrivals and go about our work, assessing their injuries, cleaning them up. They're all kids. Siblings.

None is badly hurt.

Mom's coming in with the sheriffs. We hear she ran a red light and hit an earthmover. We hear one kid was killed. The eight-year-old sister tells us the details. The kids were in the backseat. After the crash, she looked over to her little brother.

"He didn't have a head," she whimpers.

We cringe inside, horrified at what this little girl had to witness.

We try to hide our distress to the kids, to each other, and to the other patients.

We calmly offer care and comfort as though nothing unusual has happened.

Inside we are sick.

Mom arrives in custody. She was driving under the influence. Not the first time for her.

We tell her about the kids we have. We let her know they're OK. The deputies tell her about her other son.

The ER is pierced by female shrieks.

The sound is unnerving, unrelenting, chilling. It is the sound of raw grief from the depths of a shattered heart. It leaves goose bumps.

Mom is inconsolable. She screams his name. Screams denial. Screams she's sorry. Sedatives and closed doors do little to muffle her cries.

Outside the doors, we try to practice business as usual. We act as though her shrieks don't exist. Patients and visitors hear her pain and look at us questioningly. We smile reassuringly. They must think we're deaf. Some ask what's wrong and we offer some bland explanation.

The only clue to our distress is in the lack of our usual chitchat and in the looks we give each other.

Finally, she's gone—but it takes some time for her cries to leave our heads.

# OOPS!

W e are comfortable with body parts, touching,
    viewing, discussing. It's part of the job. No
big deal.

We ask people to disrobe, then listen and probe
without a second thought.

We casually discuss baseball scores and recipes
while engrossed in intimate patient contact.

Sometimes we get a little too casual, seeming to
forget just where we are.

It was noon.

The lady on the pelvic table was undressed and
draped, feet in stirrups, knees apart. Ready to be
viewed.

The nurse stood at her side.

The doctor sat on his rolling stool, speculum
poised and glistening with lubricant. He was moving into position to take a look when his stomach
gave a loud rumble. "Time to eat!" he proclaimed.

# LAB TECH

We three nurses are bustling around the gurney of an elderly, heavyset, comatose woman, assessing, administering, efficiently doing our job.

The young male lab tech at her side has just finished drawing blood when he abruptly falls forward, face in her crotch, and begins making loud snorting noises.

As a group we recoil in shock. What is he doing?

It's one of those moments that seem to last forever.

Snuffle. Snuffle. Long snort. His head trembles. Is he a pervert? What is he doing? Can't he control himself?

We look at each other in disbelief.

We look back at him. Snort. Snort.

Reason eventually penetrates our brains. We realize he has fainted and the snorts are his attempts to breathe with his nose buried in her fleshy folds.

Lying him flat on the floor produces a rapid recovery.

He makes a quick exit, totally embarrassed, muttering that he has been feeling ill all day and begging us not to tell his boss.

We don't.

# WINTER MORNING
# TRAUMA

It's a cold winter morning. The paramedic reports there are five victims—two women and three small kids.

Their car is upside down in a ditch.

The report is brief but exact. It's obvious the rescuers are swamped.

While they sort patients, we sort hospitals.

Kids One and Two sound critical. They'll fly with a doc to Children's Hospital sixty miles away. One mom and her child can go to a nearby ER—they aren't too serious.

Victim Number Five is still in the upside-down car. The paramedics figure another twenty minutes to extricate and twenty more to the regional trauma center. We hope she can make it there, and we tell the trauma team to expect her.

No go.

Though she was talking when the paramedics first got to her, their efforts to keep her going are futile. They have to watch her fade while they struggle to free her body. The trauma center's too far. She needs a closer ER.

Victim Number Five is flying to us.

She arrives, CPR in full swing. She's young. Pump the blood in. She deserves our full effort. Circulate the drugs. There's a pulse now. Check her pressure. Only a few bruises and scrapes are visible. Her chest looks OK. Get more blood.

Pulse is gone. What else can we do?

This isn't working. Has it already been an hour?

"She's the same age as me," someone says while pumping her heart.

During that hour details dribble in. The boy and girl at the trauma center are hers. They're not doing well.

She was driving and overcorrected when her wheels left the road.

Her husband is on his way here from the other ER.

We get a name. Is it really her name?

We finally stop. 11:55 A.M.

There's nothing more to do but fill out papers and prepare her for her family. In a few minutes the chaotic, bloody room is cleared.

We cover the holes where bones punctured her skin. We wash blood from her hands and lay them on top of the sheet covering her body. We place a clean pad under her head to hide the blood-soaked sheets.

We're thinking of her children—of our children.

Finally her husband's here. He's alone. He has no idea. In the family room the doc tells him. No fancy words, just that she has been killed.

We sit with him, the doc's hand on his shoulder as he sobs silently, shoulders shaking, tears dripping from his face.

I wonder if he can feel our sadness. Does it help him that we're here?

Slowly he absorbs reality, asks questions.

We explain what we know about the accident and his children.

He goes to her and the sobbing begins again. He verifies her name. He can't remember her birthday. They had breakfast together a couple of hours ago. It was raining so he hadn't gone to work.

She was traveling to pick up his mother. He was the one who was supposed to have picked up his mother.

She was three months pregnant. She had an OB appointment today.

They'd been married seven years.

He has to go to his children now. No, he can't wait for someone to go with him. We're worried about him driving sixty miles alone. OK, he'll pick up his brother. Where is the children's hospital?

He kisses her face and walks out.

We zip up the shroud. We look at each other. It's hard to believe.

In one brief morning a young family has been obliterated.

# THEY JUST KEEP COMING

And always, the show must go on.
While someone is dying in one room, the broken arms, rashes, and headaches in the other rooms are still there and need attention.
The gurneys rarely cool off.
We care about the patients.
We complain about the patients.
We like each other.
We complain about each other—we're like siblings.
We love the action. We really love the action!
We complain about the action.
And when it is slow,
We wonder what's wrong.

# P A R T
# SIX

A young man about fifteen years old was brought in awash with the feeling of dread and exhaustion that comes at the end of a methamphetamine binge. He lay on the gurney shirtless while his prim mother sat sternly at his bedside. An exam reassured me that he was in no immediate danger, but I was concerned for his future. He told me he had been injecting the "crank" in his veins. The needles were shared with his friends.

I hoped to lead him into a realization of the dangers of sharing needles. So I asked him, "Can you think of anything you have been doing that might cause you to get AIDS?"

Worry came over his face. He knew I had something in mind. With a frown, he took a moment to survey his catalog of misdeeds, searching for the correct answer. At last he brightened and looked at me, and said questioningly, "I've been fucking the dog?"

*Lightbulbs, vegetables, garden hoses, Coke bottles, silverware, pencils, money, candles, golf balls, tele-*

phones, spark plugs, paper clips, and flashlights are just a few of the things that people have come to the emergency room to have removed from their private parts. These parts are called private because our cultural approach to our sexuality requires a little mystery and gossamer. Shyness and discretion carry some allure.

But when these private parts become public and are probed and inspected under glaring light day after day, what becomes of our own sense of mystery?

# SPUD

A sixty-seven-year-old gentleman came in complaining of lower abdominal pain. He reported that he had been constipated and a friend told him that a sweet potato placed in the rectum would act as a suppository and help relieve him. About twenty-four hours after following his friend's advice, he found that the sweet potato had done nothing to relieve his constipation and now he felt even more uncomfortable.

On rectal exam I felt what could have been the tip of a sweet potato about four inches up inside the rectum. Extraction with any sharp instruments or towel clamps would have been too dangerous. We decided to place a Foley catheter up past the potato, inflate the balloon on the tip of the catheter, and then pull it out, bringing the potato along with it. While pulling on the catheter, the sweet potato moved down to the anal sphincter. The patient suddenly grunted and bore down, abruptly expelling the potato. The potato flew through the curtains surrounding the patient's bed, whizzed past a candy striper, careened across the tile floor, and came to a rest in the X-ray waiting room, where the patients eyed it suspiciously.

The potato was tracked down and captured by the nurse who was assisting in the procedure. To our surprise, the potato was eight inches long and of equal circumference. For lack of a better idea, it was carefully wrapped and sent to pathology. The patient was sent home with a mild laxative.

JAMES AUGUSTINE, M.D.
*Dayton, Ohio*

# DOGGIE-STYLE

I am the nurse in triage, screening the cases as they come in to determine their level of severity. A tall gentleman comes in and tells me he has a problem. It's August, about ninety-two degrees outside, and he has on an overcoat. When I ask what the problem is, he replies, "It's personal. I have to show you."

I take him behind a screen, where he opens his overcoat. He is naked underneath, except for his penis. On this man's penis is a dog. A live toy poodle. His penis is in the dog's butt. His problem is that he can't get it off. The dog's anal sphincter is serving as a cock ring, trapping the blood in the man's penis and causing it to swell grotesquely within the dog's body. The dog is whimpering and gasping. I go back and tell the resident. He looks tired. He's seen everything in the Emergency Department rotation. He gives the dog a muscle relaxant and pries it off. The dog is already in shock and soon dies.

I would have suggested a different way to cut the dog free. I think the wrong animal died.

CARMEN DIAZ, R.N.
*Brandon, Florida*

# LIFE AND DEATH

Two patients came in today at about the same time. Both were critical.

The first was a young man who had a history of severe allergy to almonds. He was very careful about his diet because the last time he had eaten almonds he had nearly died. Today he was again in a full allergic crisis: face red and puffy, welts covering his body, eyes swollen shut, throat closing off, lungs in spasm with wheezing, blood pressure dropping. He was suffocating and his circulation was collapsing. IVs, fluids, steroids, intravenous adrenaline—he began to turn around and do better. As he improved, I was struck by the intensity of his desire to live: heart pounding, eyes alert, fighting for breath, determined to survive. He did, and was fine. It turned out that his girlfriend had been eating baklava for lunch and had a small piece of almond stuck in her teeth. The two of them had been necking and he had been exposed to the almond. It was nearly the kiss of death.

The second was a young woman who had taken

handfuls of different drugs in an effort to end her life. She arrived in a coma, with a falling blood pressure and cardiac dysfunction. She soon went into full cardiac arrest and we were unable to revive her. She died within thirty minutes of arriving in the department. She left a suicide note that read, "If any one of you care for me, never let my daughter know what a low-life failure I was."

I was struck by the contrast of how some people cling to life while others fear the thought of facing another day.

JAMES WEBER, D.O.
*Royal Oak, Michigan*

# PISSED OFF

My first experience with emergency medicine came approximately fifteen years ago, when I was young, fresh, and thought that I could handle just about anything. At this stage of my new career, I enjoyed working nights because I found that the patients who frequented the ER during the early morning hours were a more interesting group.

It was 3 A.M. We had emptied out the ER and were looking forward to a few hours of relaxation. One of our nurses was sitting at the triage desk sorting through eighty charts from the preceding twenty-four-hour period. As she was working there, a filthy man appeared and stated that he wanted to be seen by the doctor. He was disheveled and smelled fetid and drunk. The nurse excused herself to fetch a stethoscope, and when she returned seconds later she found the would-be patient standing up on the triage desk, urinating all over the eighty charts.

I was in the ER treatment area and heard her scream. I arrived just in time to hear her reprimanding the gentleman for his lack of self-control. She was obviously upset, and speculated aloud that his parents might not be married. He subsequently told both of us to commit acts that are not anatomically possible, and stumbled out of the ER.

Once we recovered from the shock of the unpleasant encounter, we set ourselves to the task of preserving the eighty urine-soaked charts. We concluded that the best way to dry them was to lay them out one page at a time on all the available ER counter space.

Seven o'clock rolled around and the day-shift personnel began to arrive. I sat in the triage area and watched the expressions on their faces as they entered what smelled like a ballpark men's room. Knowing very well that I would be leaving for home within minutes, I jokingly taunted my coworkers with comments about working in a urinal all day. Then, one of the staff arrived and yelled out to me, "Hey, Doc! There's somebody sleeping in your Jeep."

I could feel my scrotum contract. My Jeep was a brand-new canvas-top Golden Eagle. I loved that car. I raced into the parking lot. I got to my Jeep and opened the passenger door. Cigarette smoke billowed out. There, stretched out across the front seats of my pristine automobile, slept the drooling, drunken, dirty, urine-soaked body of Mr. 3 A.M.

B. RICHARD STILES, D.O.
*West Chester, Pennsylvania*

# ADOLESCENCE

The fifteen-year-old girl averted her eyes as I entered the examining room. Grandma was fat and paced like a ferret. I had interrupted some passion play and the tension made the room seem smaller than it was.

"I'm Dr. O'Malley, what can I do for you?"

My patient didn't answer.

"Tell him what you here for. Tell him what that boy done to you."

I thought that my patient was going to throw up, but she began quietly crying. I gently asked Grandma to wait outside, and left her cussing at some paramedics in their ready room. When I returned to the examining room, my patient had stopped crying and was nervously tugging at a shoelace. She wore a T-shirt with PUBLIC ENEMY on it. I have all their CDs, and I suddenly felt very old.

My patient was an honors student. Her posture was perfect. She was enrolled in summer school for advanced college-placement credits. Her lower abdominal pain had begun several days ago, one week after her first sexual experience. He was an older boy from around the block that she knew from the neighborhood. The diagnosis wasn't particularly difficult. The disposition was.

I allowed my patient to remain clothed. I sat on a low stool in a far corner of the closet-sized room. I explained to her the intricacies of a pelvic exam—an experience I would need to introduce her to. From her position atop the exam table, she listened politely to my explanations about adnexa and cultures and specula, and gave an occasional sigh. As the conversation turned to infections, she grew deathly quiet and her attention became rapt. For a while she held her breath.

"You know, if you have sex with someone and you don't use a condom, getting pregnant isn't all you have to worry about."

"I know."

"Besides syphilis, gonorrhea, and venereal warts, there are other diseases that our . . . uh, your generation has to worry about." My patient was silent. "Do you know what disease I'm talking about?"

My patient gasped softly and began to sob. "Yes." She sniffed. "AIDS."

"Do you love this guy?"

"I don't know."

"That's OK." I asked her to undress and I went for a nurse.

When I finished, the nurse prepared the injection and I found Grandma still simmering. I sat down and offered her coffee. She declined and lit a cigarette.

"Well . . . she's pregnant, ain't she? Lord Jesus, I know that son of a bitch got her pregnant. You know that he waited for her mother to be at work and for me to be out shopping. He waited for an empty house and got that girl pregnant."

"She's not pregnant."

"She's not?"

"No. We did a test."

"Thank the Lord for that." She smashed the cig-arette out in the ashtray, gave a long sigh, and folded her hands in her lap. She no longer appeared angry, she just seemed tired.

"She has an infection."

"Gonorrhea?"

"Maybe. Probably. Listen, I know that you're an-gry, but don't be angry with her. She made a mis-take. She needs you now. If you need to be angry with someone, take it out on the guy that did this to her."

"Can I get him arrested?"

"I don't know."

Grandma thought for a minute and lit another cig-arette. I sipped my coffee and wrote up the chart. The fluorescent lights buzzed noisily overhead and drowned out the din of the Emergency Department down the hall. "Damn fool girl," Grandma said. "I could've killed her when she told me about it."

"But she told you anyway."

"Yeah."

As my patient walked down the hall, she limped slightly, sore from the gluteal injection. At first Grandma walked behind, oblivious to the girl's gait, but as they neared the exit doors I watched carefully as my patient offered her denim jacket to the old woman. Grandma put on the jacket and gently led my patient by the elbow out the door, into the softly falling summer rain. Then they took each others' hand and walked out. I felt the tightening of goose bumps on my arms and turned back into the fray.

GERALD O'MALLEY, D.O.
*New York, New York*

# SOUR GRAPES

It was a Friday in the summer of 1973 and the gastroenterologists had a new toy: a fiber-optic flexible scope, which allowed for a periscope view of the inside of the colon. It was equipped with a biopsy forceps. They let it be known to the ER staff that they would be willing, even happy, to evaluate and treat rectal bleeding in the ER. In fact, they added an incentive—a six-pack of any domestic beer—for the house officer who recruited an "appropriate" (i.e., insured) patient.

Enter Mr. Simmons. He had blood in his stool, and a GI series showed a polyp in the transverse colon. He was stable, cooperative, and insured: the perfect recruit. Three gastroenterologist attendings and a gastroenterologist fellow performed the colonoscopy in the ER pelvic room. It was not a short procedure, and there was joyful shouting when the polyp was finally located (not exactly where it seemed to be on the X ray, but then again, we were reminded, the colon is a mobile organ). The polyp was snared and gingerly extricated. I held the formalin container as the stool-coated growth was deposited during smiles and self-congratulatory handshakes. The fellow took it up to pathology himself, not trusting the precious specimen to some anonymous orderly.

The pathologist evaluated the "polyp" and issued his report on Tuesday morning. I was alone when I read the formally phrased and very brief report. I knew I'd be buying my own six-pack.

The pathology report said: "Normal grape."

MICHAEL HELLER, M.D.
*Pittsburgh, Pennsylvania*

# GUESS AGAIN

The seventy-year-old female patient had a history of frequent urinary-tract infections. She had a fever and slight back pain, so I ordered a catheterized urine specimen to be sent to the lab. I went on to other patients, but the nurse soon returned and said she had tried to cath the woman but couldn't find her urethra—the opening to the bladder. She had asked several other nurses to help her cath the lady, but no one could find the urethral opening. I decided to help, and went to the patient's bedside. I found an elderly, pleasant woman who told me about the history of frequent urinary problems and told me she was childless.

I examined the woman's perineum and identified the larger orifice of what appeared to be the vaginal vault, and searched above this for the urethral opening. I couldn't find an opening either, but as I looked, some urine trickled out of the vagina. Suspecting a fistula connecting the bladder to the vagina, or an embedded urethral meatus, I decided to look inside the vagina with a speculum. As I readied to do this, however, I noticed something underneath the vagina, on the perineum, and looked closer. I found the patient's vagina and *intact hymen* under what I had assumed was the vagina. I realized that the upper opening she was using as a vagina was in fact the patient's urethra. I asked the woman if she had any problems with sexual relations with her husband.

"Not really. It hurt the first year or so, but it was fine after that."

She had been married for fifty-two years.

CHARLES HAGEN, M.D.
*Auburn, Alabama*

# PLASTIC SURGERY

On a Sunday evening we received a call from a paramedic who said he was bringing in a woman with some nasal trauma. The patient arrived in the Emergency Department, a gauze pad covering her face. When the gauze was removed, it was noted that her nose had been removed as well—flush with her cheekbones. This included the amputation of both the soft tissues and bony tissue of the nose. The nasal concha were completely visible. Remarkably, there was absolutely no bleeding.

When the patient was asked what had happened, she told the following story:

No longer in love with her husband, she had found, and now loved, another man. She and her lover had gone to her home and explained to her husband that she was leaving and would not be back.

Her husband, who had been drinking, got up silently from the sofa, went into the bedroom, and came back into the living room with a .30 caliber rifle. The husband had the wife tie the lover's hands behind his back and lay him facedown on the living-room floor. The husband tied up the wife in the same fashion. The husband then shot the wife's boyfriend in the rectum, the exit wound nearly blowing off his genitals. The husband then proceeded to lift his wife's head off the floor by her hair and took a serrated knife and sawed the patient's nose off her face. He flushed the nose down the toilet. The husband then notified the police.

DONALD GRAHAM, M.D.
*Boring, Oregon*

# THE HEALER

I had a friend in school
thought he could save the world.
Always said he wanted to do general practice
in some hillbilly place
like the Appalachians or something.
Said he'd take chickens, or hams, or vegetables
in return for his work.
Said he'd still make house calls
and birth babies and such.

I used to laugh at him a little
although I thought he was a nice guy
with good intentions and all.

But the rest of us knew that our payoff
would come someday.
A big house with three garages
a Porsche

maybe a Rolex
and of course, respect.
Somehow chickens and hams
just didn't cut it for what they put us through.

One time late at night
when we were bone-tired from hunching over
our cadavers
tired of trying to find nerves and vessels
tired of that formaldehyde smell
that seems to stick to you wherever you go
and kills your sense of smell for anything else,
one time he told me why he wanted to be a
doctor.

I can't remember it word for word
but it was something about being a healer
about knowing that he was one.
He said he had a sixth sense about things
that he knew how to help people.
He said that when the spirit allowed
that he knew just how to touch them with his
hands
and just where, and how hard, and how long.

So he decided to become a doctor
figuring that it might be something new and
powerful
to combine his heart for the metaphysical
with a head full of scientific knowledge
of anatomy, and physiology, and modalities
and such.

He hoped for a kind of synergy, he said,
some sort of $2 + 2 = 8$ thing
where he could diagnose and treat in two di-
mensions at once
and really do the job right.

I thought it was a bit naïve
not to mention a little eccentric.
But as I've said, he was nice enough and all.
And he worked hard and learned his stuff
and did fine in school.

Although he did comment from time to time
that it was crushing his right brain
and that a certain spark seemed to be dying
and that he hadn't felt the power in his hands
for quite a while.

As the semesters rolled on
he settled in, though,
and became more like us
and told gross jokes
and laughed at some of his patients
and talked about buying a nice car someday.

And after a while he stopped talking about his
sixth sense
and just got into the work
and sweat blood over the next set of exams
just like the rest of us
and sometimes was happy just to get by
just like the rest of us.

I wonder what he's doing now.
We've lost touch.
The last time we talked
he said that he was working
in some Emergency Department in Illinois
and that he was trying to find himself.

KEITH N. BYLER, D.O.
*Edwardsville, Illinois*

# CPR

When you do CPR you get some blood flowing, but usually not enough to do more than keep the heart and brain alive for a few extra minutes. In rare cases, though, for reasons no one quite understands, you can actually provide almost normal blood flow just by pumping rhythmically on the chest.

We had such a patient once, a sixtyish man who was brought in by the paramedics in cardiac arrest. There were no family members, and we knew nothing about him.

His heart monitor showed ventricular fibrillation, which was a relatively good sign, since VFib is the only "rhythm of arrest" from which people really ever survive. Not that good, though, as only about 10 percent of people with VFib ever leave the hospital.

Shortly after he arrived, with CPR in progress, we were startled to see him open his eyes. With a breathing tube down his throat he couldn't talk, but he was clearly conscious. The CPR was keeping enough blood moving to his brain.

We checked the monitor just to be sure, but it really did still show VFib, and in fact, when we stopped CPR in order to do the check, the patient passed out again. Once we started up again, though, he rapidly responded and even seemed to make eye contact with the people above him.

CPR must be painful, but it's nothing compared to defibrillation, the big jolt of electrical energy we use for VFib. Ordinarily this doesn't seem relevant, since patients we shock like this are already comatose (if not, in some way, already dead). But this man was looking at us!

We had to do it, though, because VFib is not compatible with continued survival. And we didn't think it would be smart to give him any sedatives or pain medicines, because they all have suppressive effects on the heart. So we stopped CPR, and thankfully, while we were positioning the paddles, his eyes rolled back into his head and he went out before we shocked him.

Most patients respond to defibrillation by getting better (developing useful electrical activity) or getting worse (losing all electrical activity), but this man stayed the same, with VFib still on the monitor. We shocked him repeatedly, ultimately using the maximal current, and trying all our adjunctive drugs as well, but no matter what we did, his heart stayed in VFib.

And he stayed in the same extraordinary place not only between life and death, but between consciousness and death. Every time we did CPR, he opened his eyes and seemed to look into each of our eyes. And every time we stopped, even for a few seconds, he died.

With each shock the smell of his burned chest increased, and we were sure he was in agony each time he awoke. Although we usually call off our efforts if they've failed for a half hour or so (since when we succeed it's invariably in the first few minutes of CPR), we kept trying, and shocking, for two hours.

We had to keep going, because unlike so many patients in whom the sense of humanness is lost as they go through the act of dying, this man kept looking at us. He couldn't communicate or answer our questions, but the more we worked on him the more obvious it was that he was alert and even seemed to know that he was dying. And the more we worked on him, the more each one of us felt, as we acknowledged later, that he was looking right at "me," that he was depending on each "me" among us to save him.

But none of our efforts worked, and over time it became more and more obvious that saving him just wasn't going to happen. If we changed positions so someone could get a breather from doing CPR, he died, and when we started up again, he was reborn! There was a temptation to stop on purpose for a few seconds, almost like a game, to witness this remarkable event. We also felt, with each successive effort, an increasing dread of subjecting him to another defibrillation.

Finally, with the whole team exhausted, the ER backing up with other patients, and hope of success completely gone, we had to stop the resuscitation. We couldn't keep this up forever; it was futile, it was crazy. So we had to stop pumping on the chest of a man who was looking at us, knowing that when we did he would be dead. We could just stop, and he'd be dead soon enough. Or we could tell him.

One of the hardest things in medicine is telling a parent, or a spouse, or anyone, that someone he or she loves is dead. It's particularly hard in the ER, because you usually know neither the one who died nor the survivors. This was the first and only time, though, that I had to tell a patient himself. That I had to say, "We are going to stop trying, for reasons of our own, and you will die." I didn't use those words, of course, but I couldn't keep from feeling that that was the underlying message, pure and simple.

I touched him, and said the most comforting things I could think of (even while someone else kept whaling on his chest so he could live through these eerie last moments). I tried to get him to communicate with me, to tell me if he wanted something, to forgive me, to curse me. Anything. But he didn't. He just kept looking at my eyes. Finally, I told him one more time, and then, a few seconds later, we stopped the CPR.

I've always wondered what he was thinking. Did he really understand what was going on? Was there something he wanted to say before it was over, or someone he wanted to say it to? Was he terrified that we'd stop, or terrified that we'd continue? Were his eyes begging me to keep him alive, or, please, just to let him die?

Twenty years later, I still think of him from time to time. And I still don't have a clue.

JEROME R. HOFFMAN, M.D.
*Los Angeles, California*

# IN THE FAMILY

From 1984 to 1991, I served as staff physician and medical director for the Yosemite Medical Clinic in Yosemite National Park. Although not a hospital, the clinic is the sole source of medical care for almost all of the twelve thousand square miles that make up Yosemite.

The summer is the busy season. I was on duty with one of my associates on a typical July day in 1988; we had only just begun and already there was a three-hour wait for nonemergency problems. We received a call on the radio that park medics were en route by helicopter from the Tenaya Lake campground with an unresponsive infant. CPR was in progress for the three-month-old female, who was not breathing and pulseless.

She was one of four children—the daughter her father had always wanted. She seemed fine that morning when she had been put down for a nap in the family tent while her parents made breakfast. They were only a few feet away and had been out of the tent less than five minutes when her mother returned to find her cold, pale, and lifeless.

The father was a well-established cardiologist with a group practice in Southern California. The mother was an ICU nurse. They immediately started CPR on their little girl while someone ran to call for assistance. The child was still apneic and pulseless as she was being loaded into the helicopter for transport. Flight time to our clinic was five to ten minutes. Flight time to a hospital of any size from Tenaya Lake was a minimum of thirty minutes.

We set up our one-bed ER with all that the clinic had available for an infant resuscitation. One of the nurses came to me and said, "They're here," and I vividly recall the gut-wrenching feeling I experienced knowing I was walking into a disaster. The child was mottled, cool, pulseless, and the monitor showed flatline. Intubation went smoothly, but we could not establish an IV. Dad arrived as I was working on a cutdown.

He was a large man—five to six inches taller than me and at least fifty pounds heavier. He could best be described as being in a state of controlled panic. When he realized that an IV had not been successfully established, he picked up equipment and made several attempts to start central venous lines himself. There was absolutely no way to persuade him to leave the room. We could not physically remove him—there was no one big enough to do so. After about twenty minutes, he finally gave in and joined his family in the waiting room. Resuscitation was terminated about forty-five minutes from the time of arrival.

The local priest had been called. After we stopped the resuscitation, I went out to look for the father. He was wandering around outside the building followed by the priest. My associate had gone back to start seeing other patients. Park medics had already been called away to another incident. I finally caught up to the father and he asked, "Is she gone?" When I said "Yes," we hugged each other and cried together.

The following year, a woman in her late sixties was brought to the clinic in severe respiratory distress. She was initially attended to by a nurse and a respiratory therapist who were camping at the next campsite. The two followed the patient to the clinic to learn the outcome. I spoke to them and thanked them for their help. The nurse commented to her friend that she knew a cardiologist whose daughter had died in the clinic the year before. As it turned out, she was referring to the infant flown to us from Tenaya Lake.

I had not been in touch with the baby's parents during the year following her death. I got their address from the nurse and wrote to the father. He soon wrote back saying he and his wife had had another child—a boy. The painful memories of the previous year so far prevented him and his family from returning to Yosemite; however, he hoped to be able to do so sometime in the future.

In my seven years in Yosemite, I participated in a total of six SIDS resuscitations. In five of those six cases, I felt that I was somehow able to maintain the balance of caring, compassion, and professionalism that comes with time. This case, however, was the worst and most devastating code in which I have ever been involved. The fact that the parents were physician and nurse—my colleagues, my professional family—seemed to drive the pain of this case much deeper. I still cry when I think about it.

GARY M. FLASHNER, M.D.
*Wapwallopen, Pennsylvania*

# ALONE

At 4 A.M. the ER was finally quiet, except for the interrupted snores and snorts coming from room E, where the sole patient was dreaming drunken dreams after being "rescued" by emergency personnel from his pile of beer cans. Because in Utah the beer has only 3.2 percent alcohol content, it takes a case, drunken with swiftness and commitment, to get to the prized level of near-insensate stupor. I had to lean over a large yellow puddle to shake his shoulder. He grunted a somewhat underwater "Huh?" coughed once, then drifted back to his own, preferred world. Satisfied, I pulled up the blanket. The snore became muffled as I walked away.

"Here's a call from someone who wants to speak only with the doctor." Katie was holding the phone like it was a dead snake. I reached for it and drew up a chair at the long white desk. I have never liked "advice" calls because they take the staff's time away from the patients. Especially at night they tend toward the macabre. This was no exception.

"Are you the doctor?" It was a whispering, feminine voice. "Is this totally confidential?"

"I can barely hear you. Yes, yes, go ahead."

"I have to be quiet because my husband is in bed next to me sleeping." The whisper held anxiety.

"I'm calling because my husband has AIDS and I just today got my test result back." A pause. "It was positive." Her voice choked, then became a monotone. "I don't know what to do."

"Have you gotten any counseling?"

"Noooo." Silence, then: "Also, I'm pregnant and I've started to bleed. I . . . I want to keep this baby." She began to cry quietly.

"Why don't you come in and we can talk about it?" Suddenly I felt very alert.

"I can't. You see, I work at the hospital. I'm a medical student. If anyone found out about me being HIV positive, I'd be kicked out of school and never be able to get a residency or a job. . . .But I feel like I need to tell someone."

"Have you told your husband any of this?"

"No." A sob, interrupted by silence. "You know, he was promiscuous. He got AIDS from a friend. I came home one night, early. And there he was in bed with another man. He told me he could sleep with whoever he wanted. He wants me to engage in anal intercourse, but I won't because it's not right."

"That's quite a burden you're carrying around with you. Why don't you come in tonight? No one else will know you've been here, just myself and the crisis worker."

"I just want to feel better. I have twenty Percocets here. What would happen if I took them?"

"You know you'd hurt yourself. Are you threatening to hurt yourself?" I was beginning to feel manipulated. This wasn't getting anywhere.

"I'm just asking you what I should do."

"If you come in, I can help you. Otherwise, I can't."

"You're not very understanding, Doctor. Sorry I bothered you." With a click, her voice was gone. I looked at the white telephone in my hand, then placed it softly in its plastic cradle. I slid a new pen from the drawer, stared at it, and began to chart, wondering if I'd ever hear from her again. The next evening, while walking through the ER waiting room:

"Excuse me, are you the doctor?"

I knew it was the woman who had called. She had large, liquid eyes with brown pupils wide open, like a cat caught in the headlights of an onrushing car. Dark brown hair was pulled back, with a few tousled hairs meeting generous eyebrows. She wore pale green scrubs with trouser legs taped back in OR style. The V-top revealed two thin, gold chain necklaces which disappeared between the sides of two pale breasts. She wore a scrub gown loosely over her shoulders, like a shawl, only like a shawl designed by the Army. She pulled it tight over her chest with one hand, as if sensing a cool draft of night air. The movement revealed the curvature of her small breasts and flatness of her abdomen. She had the smooth skin of someone in her early twenties. Not a cat, I thought. She looked like nothing so much as a kitten waiting to be let in on a December night, tired and scared.

I suddenly wanted to put my arm around her.

"Come in, come in, what can I do for you?" I opened a door to the treatment area.

"Do you have a few minutes? In private? I don't want to hold you if you've got someone you have to see." I looked at the names on the board and fought the urge to be truthful.

"Should I come back later?"

I motioned her into a room. She closed the door, but sat next to it. I sat facing her. She leaned forward and stared at me with a dazed look and began to smile somewhat vacantly.

"I've got a question for you that I've never asked anyone before," she said. I leaned forward. "Are you involved?"

"Yes," I lied. The silence became uncomfortable. "I'm married."

"I was going to ask if you'd like to go with me to the symphony tomorrow. Would you like to go anyway?"

"Are you the one who called last night?"

"Yes." She looked downward, but for only a moment.

"Would you keep this confidential?" She reached into her backpack and produced an envelope addressed to me, only with my name spelled phonetically. "I'd like it back when you've read it."

The handwriting was minuscule and the lines overlapped, but it was impossible to ignore the seductiveness of phrases such as "I want to be your lover....You are so compassionate and understanding. . . ." It went on and on. I felt uncomfortable to be reading it.

She was smiling and looking at me. She brushed back her hair in a coquettish way. She was very attractive. She was waiting for an answer, but I could not translate my feelings into words. For a moment, it was tempting. Then I thought, that's all I need right now is an affair with a married medical student who is pregnant. Then I recalled what she said the night before—with HIV.

"Was that true what you said about being HIV positive and a medical student and being pregnant and bleeding?" I sort of blurted it out.

"I wish it wasn't," she said. Then I noticed that

her hands were scarred, like I had seen in crisis patients who must physically abuse themselves to "let out the tension."

"I just need a friend right now," she said plaintively. She began moving toward me.

I doubted that friendship was all she wanted. "I don't feel worthy of your affection or competent to counsel you. Would you stay and speak with someone who's trained in how to approach problems like yours?"

With a feline movement, her hand was on the doorknob. "I can't stay, but I'll leave you messages about how I'm doing." In a flash of pale green, she was gone.

I felt dazed and sad. I was drawn to her and felt that I'd blown it by being professional when she wanted a friend, by thinking of her as a patient rather than as a woman. Suddenly I wanted to find her again, to tell her that I cared and wanted to go out with her. The dean's office would have her picture and from that I could get her name and telephone number. If I did, I knew that my personal involvement with her would not stop at having dinner or attending the symphony. Why was the thought of pleasing her as a man so exciting? Was it the poignancy of loving someone doomed to a premature, unnatural death?

I never found out who she was. She never left any messages. But I saw her again, two years later, in the reception area for lawyers' offices. I was reading the newspaper while a contract was being reviewed when I heard a soft, whispering voice.

"Is anyone sitting there?" She indicated the chair next to mine. I motioned for her to sit, but was not able to place her for a few minutes. Her hair was drawn in a bun. She was wearing a gold necklace, white blouse, and dark slacks. She was still as attractive as when I saw her in scrubs, but looked less tentative, more self-assured and purposeful. She returned my look without emotion.

"Do you remember me?" I asked. "We spoke on the telephone, then met in the emergency room." Her cheeks began to flush in recall.

"Well, how are you?" I asked.

She told me she was suing someone. At that moment, the receptionist announced that she could go in to see her attorney.

I have never seen her again, and never discovered whom she was suing. Maybe her husband, for giving her AIDS. She no longer looked vulnerable or afraid, perhaps because she and a lawyer were representing her interests. I felt simultaneously satisfied that she had become empowered, and sad that she had left me out of her life.

From that one early morning telephone call, I will always regret that one woman would not let me be her doctor and that I could not let myself be her friend.

ROBERT D. HERR, M.D.
*Salt Lake City, Utah*

# P A R T
# SEVEN

It was a quiet night and the nurses were sitting around the central work area drinking coffee and eating doughnuts. The doctor went to see the lone patient who had come in for rectal bleeding. The doctor's job was to put his finger up the patient's fanny and get some stool on the tip of his rubber glove, then smear a sample of the stool onto a testing card to see if it contained blood. He put on his rubber glove, disappeared into the patient's room, smeared chocolate frosting onto the gloved fingertip, returned to the central work area, sat down with the nurses, and licked off the tip of his brown-tipped finger.

"Tastes like blood, all right," he announced.

When the press of patients subsides, and the relative quiet allows the staff to relax and let their guard down, it calls forth the second most ancient pastime of the Pit: making fun of each other.

# TURF

Turf: to transfer to another facility a troublesome patient.

One quickly learns how to "turf" in the ER. A gentleman in his seventies was brought in by his wife for worsening leg edema. The patient also suffered from organic brain syndrome (Alzheimer's), making it difficult to obtain any history. The wife kept insisting that the patient was a World War II veteran and he should be transferred to the VA hospital. We called the VA and informed them that we would be transferring this patient. One of my colleagues decided to cement the transfer by placing a sign around the patient's neck stating that he was a World War II veteran. We congratulated one another for successfully turfing the patient.

Toward the end of the shift, we saw our patient "bounce back" to the ER. He still had the sign around his neck, but there was a different message. It now read: NICE TRY. RIGHT WAR, WRONG SIDE!

Upon further questioning of the wife, we found out that the patient had fought on the side of the Germans.

DAVID B. LEVY, D.O.
*Pittsburgh, Pennsylvania*

# OWL'S WELL

On a quiet evening in our Emergency Department, the ambulance radio crackled to life: "This is Ellwood unit nine-five en route to your location. We have an eleven-year-old male with an awl attached to his arm." Thinking some type of tool had penetrated the boy's arm, I nonetheless asked them to repeat, as the story sounded peculiar. I asked if they had said "awl" or "owl," and much to my amazement came the reply, "Owl. O-w-l!"

Two minutes later, the crew wheeled in a frightened young boy with a live young screech owl perched on his forearm, talons clamped firmly, and looking as petrified as the boy. Initial attempts to simply lift it off resulted in the owl tightening its grip and the boy screaming in pain. I not only was trying to separate the two, but hoped to prevent the comic nightmare of an owl flying free in our ER. Finally, while an assistant held the bird's body and wings, I was able to unfurl the talons using a hemostat. My assistant had to grab each talon as it was released to prevent the owl from latching back on.

The boy had only a few superficial puncture wounds, and the bird was unharmed.

The owl was returned to the original scene by the ambulance crew and set free. The boy was also set free, and as he skipped off into the night was heard to exclaim, "Owl's well that ends well."

DAVID J. SIMON, M.D.
*Pittsburgh, Pennsylvania*

# THE ANGEL OF DEATH

The Angel and I are close acquaintances—perhaps friends, or even colleagues. We work at cross-purposes. We each have a job to do. With fifty years of contact—thirty years in the Army and twenty in the Pit—we have been involved together in more cases than I care to count. Ultimately, the Angel wins, but until the clock stops for the final score, I am willing to contend with him. Once, I beat him out of a sure thing by making him laugh.

One night in the Pit, things settled down to almost nothing at about 0300, and I went outside to stretch and smoke a cigar. Up drove an aging and worn Volvo. A woman—young but also worn—was lying in the reclining front passenger seat. She answered my question readily enough: "Vaginal bleeding." As I pulled the seat erect to help her out, she went unconscious—now that's orthostatic hypotension with a vengeance. I got her into a wheelchair and rolled her in with what the Supreme Court once described as "deliberate speed" so as not to alarm her husband any more than necessary. I slowed down at the nurses' desk to announce, "I'm putting this vaginal bleed into room sixteen. Call GYN stat." Rooms 5 and 6 are the GYN rooms, room 16 is the resuscitation suite. My resident got the clue and was on my heels when we entered. She took a quick look and said, "Her pad is not soaked through, but you said she was bleeding like a stuck hog?"

"No, I said she is breathing like a stuck hog."

When it comes time to butcher hogs, you cut both carotid arteries, and they do bleed a lot, but in a few seconds unconsciousness takes over and they quit struggling. Until they die, though, they point their noses up to fight for air, because they have too little blood left to carry oxygen. The resident got the picture immediately, and did a fine job of resuscitation. GYN did respond stat. She was in the OR within minutes.

I knew they would save her, for when I made the remark "breathing like a stuck hog," I heard a soft chuckle, felt a little swish of air, and got a whiff of sweat and feathers as the Angel turned and left.

DOUGLAS LINDSEY, M.D.
*Tucson, Arizona*

# SAY WHAT?

One of the nurses who was picking up dirty linen noticed a pink wad of gum on a bedside table. She grabbed a paper towel, picked up the disgusting thing, and threw it in the trash. When the patient returned to his room from X-ray, he asked, "Has anyone seen my Miracle Ear?"

MYKA CLARK, R.N.
*Green Bay, Wisconsin*

# SO WHAT ELSE IS NEW?

Not everyone reacts to pelvic exams in the same manner. I've noticed that many women tune out conversations or questions until the exam is over. In one such case, while the patient was in stirrups, the physician asked, "Are you sexually active with more than one partner?" The patient was staring at the wall, seemingly oblivious to the question. I was the nurse assisting the exam, and I touched her shoulder to bring her back to the conversation. She looked startled and said, "Oh, I thought he was talking to you."

BRENDA HILL, R.N.
*Syracuse, New York*

# BAPTISM

Prior to going to medical school I worked as a paramedic. We were dispatched one Saturday afternoon to a woman with a reported miscarriage. Upon arrival, we found the fire department EMTs already on the scene. They reported that the woman had induced an abortion with a coat hanger, and that the fetal remains were in the corner, covered with a towel. The woman was in shock, with a rapid heartbeat and marked hypotension as well as active vaginal bleeding. We followed trauma protocol and transported her to the local Catholic hospital, where she was taken immediately to the operating room for repair of massive vaginal lacerations. The EMTs had wrapped the aborted fetus in blue pads and brought that to the hospital as well.

As we were completing our paperwork, the hospital's priest came into the ER. He went to the dirty utility room where the wrapped fetus had been placed. The priest baptized the fetus, anointing the blood-soaked towels with holy water, and then withdrew, leaving the charge nurse to handle the remains. The nurse put on gloves and, with a grim expression and a large pathology specimen-bucket, went into the dirty utility room. She carefully unwrapped the towel and blue pads from around the fetus, and paused. We watched her carefully inspect the specimen. She called a colleague in for consultation. Their examination was followed by an intense, low-voiced conversation. Finally, the nurse came to us and reported that what the woman had removed from her vagina with a coat hanger was, in fact, a swollen tampon.

To this day, the thought of a priest administering the ritual of baptism to a tampon never fails to bring a smile to my face.

EDWARD T. DICKINSON, M.D.
*Menands, New York*

# AT THE MOVIES

About 1 A.M. I took a radio call from one of our paramedic units, at a downtown theater. The paramedics described a middle-aged male who had been struck in the head and robbed while in the lobby of the theater. All throughout their report I could hear low moaning in the background. At the conclusion of their evaluation they recommended to treat and release because the patient "was in no distress." Puzzled, I said that it didn't sound like the patient was in no distress because of all the moaning that I was hearing. They replied, "That's not the patient. We're at an X-rated theater and that's coming from the screen."

JAMES DOUGHERTY, M.D.
*Akron, Ohio*

# A LITTLE PRICK

I was treating a very scared twenty-year-old female with an inflamed vaginal cyst. The nurse, Pat, was holding her hand and trying to comfort her as I was preparing to cut and drain the cyst. With her spread legs up in the stirrups, I positioned myself between them. As I was about to inject a local anesthetic with a small syringe, Pat told my patient, "OK, now you're going to feel a little prick between your legs." After a pause, the three of us started laughing, which was just the medicine needed to get the patient to relax.

MICHAEL S. ZBIEGIEN, M.D.
*Farmington Hills, Michigan*

# THE PRONOUNCEMENT

E mergency physicians are frequently asked by police and funeral home personnel to examine and pronounce someone dead. A quick listen with the stethoscope to confirm absence of heart sounds, a look at the dilated pupils, and a feel for rigor mortis is all that it usually takes to complete the physician's task.

But on this particular day, the police grabbed everyone's attention by announcing that they had twin fetuses for pronouncement in the back of their paddy wagon. They were found lying together underneath a park bench. Reactions from the Emergency Department staff ranged from sorrow to disgust to curiosity. As the physician on duty, it was with a combination of these emotions that I followed the officers out to their vehicle.

The big steel doors opened, and there, wrapped in a sheet, were two lifeless little bodies appearing to be of approximately five months gestation.

"Who could have done such a thing?" one of the officers said. "We're looking for the mother."

I examined them a little closer and noticed something peculiar. They had hair on both sides of their noses. Also, their fingers and toes were not well formed. Finally, each had a long appendage near the buttocks.

"Gentlemen," I said, "the mother you should be looking for is a cat."

WILLIAM MALONEY, M.D.
*Evanston, Illinois*

# SHORT TAKES III

Since we are a teaching hospital, it's sometimes necessary for the same exam to be done repeatedly by medical student, resident, and attending physician. After the third rectal exam on a trauma patient, the patient stated, "I'm beginning to feel like I am in prison with my face to the shower wall."

A nineteen-year-old female was being triaged. She stated that she and her boyfriend were having sex and the condom came off but she wasn't able to retrieve it with her fingers. She went to the bathroom and "gagged myself to vomit but couldn't vomit it up either."

A Vietnamese girl who was obviously pregnant came into the ER unable to speak English and voice her complaint. The doctor rushed the patient into the GYN room and did a pelvic. When the translator was on the phone, she let us know that the patient had come in about her cough.

SHARON WISE, R.N.
*St. Louis, Missouri*

# PLAYING CHICKEN

About ten years ago I saw an intoxicated, obnoxious, elderly woman with a fracture-dislocation of the shoulder. After diagnosing her problem, we parked her gurney in the hallway and called the orthopedic surgeon to come in and take care of her. After some noisy, drunken complaining, she dozed off for a couple of hours.

The hospital blood bank had started a blood drive that day with the motto, "Don't be chicken, donate blood." A large chicken, similar to Big Bird of *Sesame Street*, came through the Emergency Department with a group of people, including the press and the administration. The chicken walked up to this lady and patted her on the shoulder and said, "Hi!" From her drunken stupor, the lady looked up at the chicken and yelled: "I've waited two hours for an orthopedic surgeon and all I get is a fucking chicken?"

BRENT D. AMEY, M.D.
*Odessa, Florida*

# P A R T
# EIGHT

*Emergency physicians leave their specialty at a higher rate than any other specialty. They burn out. A major reason they burn out is the wearing effect of being on the receiving end of a stream of human misfortune. They have no control over the rate of flow—sometimes a trickle, sometimes a flood. Whatever the doors bring.*

*Another reason is the nights. The Emergency Department never closes. No other medical specialty spends half of their practice at night. Ask a cop or janitor. Nights grind a person down over the years, pushing against the body's clock, locking one out of step with family and friends. Sleep deprivation.*

*Also, the unique population of patients seen in an Emergency Department takes its toll. If a person is too sick, or too drunk, or too nasty, or too stupid, or too crazy to get medical care in a doctor's office or clinic, that patient ends up in the emergency room. We reserve the right to refuse service to no one.*

As the years go by, the skin gets thicker, the nights get longer, and the patients get meaner. In response, the jokes get louder, the sarcasm becomes harsher, the care becomes business.

Burnout.

# BURNING OUT:
# THE LETTERS OF QUINN

---

### 1

Dear Larry,

I'm typing this letter to you on the train to work, using my new laptop. It takes about an hour on the Long Island Rail Road to Penn Station. A shorter subway ride takes me to the doors of the emergency room at St. Alban's Hospital. It's hard to believe three years have passed since my move from the city to the suburbs. Even with the commute, I still prefer it to living in Brooklyn. I think it was the fifth break-in in one year that helped me decide to leave. The dual forces of rising income and rising crime are very effective motivators to move to the suburbs. It is sad, though, to be driven from your birthplace.

I know the city well and still enjoy it, but somewhat less than when I came to work in this emergency room. Sometimes I feel my job's like that of a cop. My employment brings me in regular contact with the worst New York has to offer, and it makes me rethink the romance of the city and its citizens.

Right now we're fully staffed with five attending physicians (including me), two surgical residents, three medical residents, and a variable number of interns and medical students. It's hard to imagine that we see over eighty thousand patients per year, though lately it often feels like more.

When I enter the ER in the morning, I always ask the night shift, "How was it?" This is both out of courtesy and augury. The ancient Romans would look to the flight of birds (remember that high school Latin *bonis avibus* or *avi sinistra*) or the entrails of animals to predict the coming day. A quiet night shift augurs well; a busy night shift means pain and suffering through the day. By corollary, if someone were to say, "Gee, it's quiet today," everyone would groan, knowing that this statement is sure to bring several ambulances full of very sick "train wrecks." These beliefs have no logical basis but are firmly held dicta by most of the staff. It's an ER thing.

A couple days ago, I started my morning with a rape exam. This sixteen-year-old girl from the Midwest got off the train at Penn Station and within fifteen minutes had met a middle-aged man. He told her he was a musician and offered to give her a free guitar lesson. I guess she felt lucky because she had heard that New Yorkers were cold and unfriendly. And here she was, just off the train, and already she had a new friend. So she followed her new friend to an abandoned building . . . and guess what? No music lesson! Just rape, sodomy, and beating. It was sad, but I really couldn't believe that someone could be so naïve. The first person she met she followed to an abandoned building? Doesn't she watch television? This isn't Kansas.

This morning I see one of my fellow attendings on the train. He is engrossed in an LSAT review book. It is his notion that if he can go to law school, the

MD/JD combination will spell easy street. He wants a nice office, with a nicer salary and not as many headaches and heartaches as the ER. He is not alone in his quest. Most everyone harbors fantasies of leaving for a less stressful job. Many colleagues are consultants to the pharmaceutical industry, advertising agencies, and Wall Street analysts. I feel that one job is enough for me right now, although from time to time, when I want to give myself a headache or need money for approaching holidays, I work per diem shifts in another ER. But usually the work at St. Alban's is so overwhelming that I need every day off to recover.

More later,
Campion

## II

Dear Larry,

Remember what I said about *avi sinistra* (evil birds) and asking the night shift how it was? Well, today the belief proved true. I had arrived at work about as carefree and lighthearted as I can get. (My mother always said, "Better presumption than despair.") That was soon to change.

I said good morning to Dr. Sanchez from the night shift. He is a recent graduate of St. Alban's internal medicine program, and is still filled with the energy and enthusiasm that left me years ago. He has a wife and a pretty little daughter that he mentions a lot as he shows her picture all around. He is generally a very happy man—but not today. Needing a shave and a remedy for dark circles, he barely mumbled a good morning. I looked over his shoulder to the code room. A body was being wrapped in a shroud by the night shift nurses. The floor and walls were covered with blood. Used chest tubes and Pleur-

evacs were floating in IV fluid on the stained lino-
leum. Dr. Sanchez had the same blood covering the
bottom of his shoes and splattering his pants. I
asked, "What happened?"

Sanchez washed his hands in the sink, muttering
under his breath about the soap containers being
empty again. "That asshole in there got himself
shot," he said flatly.

"The story is, he was just standing on the corner,
minding his own business, and was shot six times
in the chest and neck at close range. His friends
show up an hour later and swear that he was a
clean-living guy and didn't have an enemy in the
world. They asked if they could spend some time
alone with him."

"Was he really an innocent bystander?" I asked.

"Are you fucking kidding?" His laugh was hu-
morless. "He had over three thousand dollars in
fives and tens, a bag full of crack vials, and a nine
millimeter pistol stuffed in his jacket pocket. No
doubt a business competitor shot him. His friends
were carrying pistols. They wanted the time alone
to lift his merchandise. They were all dirtbags," he
spat. "If not for this," he jerked his chin toward the
body covered in the white plastic shroud, "I could
have gotten an hour's sleep."

We made rounds after collecting the day's residents, interns, and medical students. Sanchez mumbled comments about the patients lying on the
stretchers. Although the ER director describes these
as "teaching rounds," there is little or no teaching
going on. This is work, and the sooner we finish
rounds the sooner the night people can go home. A
typical report goes, "This is an AIDS player with
PCP, treated with AZT and DDI in the past. He's
presented with SOB, and temp of thirty-nine C. We
did a CBC, UA, CXR, started IV Bactrim, and are

waiting for a bed. [Doctors love abbreviations.] The floor residents were assholes all night and said they couldn't find him one."

The patients are seen first in the waiting room by a triage nurse who interviews them from behind bullet-proof glass. On the basis of this assessment they either wait or come in immediately. It's not a great system. People are often reluctant to shout the intimate details of their medical problems to the nurse in the middle of a crowded waiting room. As a result, it is difficult to get an appreciation for a case when you first read the chart. We are often surprised by the differences between the stated complaint and the real complaint.

We often have several homeless residents of Penn Station in the waiting room. After being triaged for various complaints, they find one of the more comfortable straight-back cushionless plastic chairs that are bolted to the floor in the waiting room and fall asleep. Intoxicated as they are, they sleep soundly across several chairs, not hearing when their name is called for treatment, or conversely they wake and answer to their name or a name that sounds like their name, or to any name for that matter if they are drunk enough. As a result, we get false histories on many of them, pull all the wrong charts, and order all the wrong lab tests and X rays. It creates quite a mess and wastes a lot of time. When we ask why they responded to the wrong name, the usual answer is, "I dunno," or "I didn't remember my name," or "I was in a hurry." Ain't it sad.

Many people like this come to the ER in the cold weather. Hoping to avoid the homeless shelter, they present themselves with some complaint that they hope will rate an admission. Some are quite adept at malingering, and know just what to say to gain a night in the hospital. Some favorites are, "I have crushing chest pain." Or, "I can't see out of my right eye." And, "I have kidney stones." These require CT scans, IVPs, and a host of other expensive tests, not to mention physician and nurse time. There is no disincentive for them when they come to the ER. Some of them will try several times a night in different hospitals or on different shifts in the same hospital. This allows them to work on their story, hoping that a new complaint will be the open sesame to a warm hospital bed and free meals. They know that once in the hospital it is difficult to get thrown out, with the Patient's Bill of Rights posted everywhere and the Patient's Rights Advocates ready to do battle against staff who have the temerity to try and discharge someone just because he doesn't have a medical problem.

Actually, I'm getting well acquainted with all the residents of Penn Station. After I've Kwelled them for lice, sutured their head cuts, pumped their stomachs, etc., we meet several hours later in the station when they ask me for "a dolla." When I remind them I'm the doctor who just treated them for free, they say, "Oh, how about five dolla."

Just before I left to go home tonight there was a shoot-out in Chinatown that kept me overtime. Apparently a gang-related incident. The paramedics told me they had to step over many bodies to get to the people who were screaming. One member of a rival gang had entered a disco and shot an Uzi into the crowd in hopes that one of the bullets would find an opposing gang member. Three were DOA. One head injury died in the OR. Two chest wounds and several minor extremity wounds did OK. The police arrived in force with radios going and pads and pens out. As usual, they asked for my name but wouldn't tell me why. They always take control of all the phones and desk space in the ER, which makes it impossible to do any work.

I received a response to my inquiry about the Royal Flying Doctor Service. They said I would first have to register with the Australian Medical Service. I discovered they are completely funded by charity, so the rumor of big bucks is groundless. I don't know how I'd do in the air. I'd be permanently on Dramamine, I'm afraid. Anyway, Cathy and I are becoming more intertwined, so Australia doesn't look as inviting.

Write soon,
Campion

### III

Dear Larry,

Yesterday while working in the ER, I had the pleasure of dabbling in another related field: the fascinating world of dentistry. Mr. Rangoon, formerly a native of Sri Lanka, now a denizen of Washington Square Park, came into the Emergency Room with the right side of his face quite swollen. Being an astute physician, I was aware of some indisputable facts. He was poor, uneducated, hungry, and unwashed. His long shaggy hair was the home to an entire civilization of lice, and his veins were thrumming with alcohol and cocaine. He had the wild-eyed stare of those wakened suddenly from a sound sleep. A few sentences of garbled communication, and all my suppositions were confirmed. His breath was truly fetid. In the past I have not flinched at the rancid odor of tampons lost for months in cavernous vaginas (toxic box syndrome). I have confronted rotting feet of the homeless that have not seen the sunshine (let alone soap and water) for years (toxic sock syndrome). But just talking to him in an enclosed space brought tears to my eyes. He was febrile and perspiring like the proverbial pig. He looked sick and was in pain. He admitted that the cocaine was wearing off, and he no longer had the resources to replenish his supply. My empathy threatened to increase my flow of tears.

As he spoke in his interesting version of pidgin English and homeboy argot, my attention was drawn to his mouth. His teeth were cracked and yellow-brown, and looked like rotting wharf wood. They moved in their sockets as he spoke, to and fro with every breath or movement of the tongue. I told him to sit down. There were no empty chairs, so he sat on top of the garbage can. I put on a pair of latex gloves and examined his mouth with a flashlight. It was a sight to give a periodontist nightmares. His teeth (such as they were) were surrounded with angry red mounds of gum tissue, each mound issuing gouts of green pus with little or no provocation. This sight, added to the overpowering stench, nearly had me running to the bathroom.

I wondered: His teeth look so loose, will they come out if I give them some encouragement? Ever the intrepid doctor, I looked at my gloved hand, considered the mess that was his mouth, and put on another glove. I asked him to open his mouth and told him not to bite. I promised myself that I would stop if he started to scream (or I started to scream) and call a dentist. (Though I knew of no dentist who was likely to leave his lucrative practice to rush over here and look at this mess.) I thrust my hand into his festering maw and firmly grasped his remaining front teeth. I could feel how loose they were, though they felt like they were connected with string. I gave a solid, confident yank, and out came three teeth with several cupfuls of pus and blood. Boy, was that satisfying! His facial swelling was going down already. Mr. Rangoon sat calmly, seeming to take all

this with equanimity. Encouraged by his lack of ob-
jection, I continued to pull the remaining teeth from
his head. They all came out with little problem except for one stubborn molar in the top back. I looked
around the ER for something like a set of pliers that
I could use to remove it, but in a rare lucid moment,
I stopped to think, and changed my mind.

I looked at Mr. Rangoon and realized suddenly
that untoothing him might be cause for some concern. He was sitting on the garbage can, drooling
blood and pus. His chin was much closer to his nose,
and he seemed to have aged thirty years in a few
minutes. He really couldn't speak well at all, and
when he did, the garbled communication was accompanied by a mist of blood and saliva that was
sprayed all over the room. So I didn't encourage
much talking. He was a very sad sight indeed.

My anxiety level rose. Did I need a consent to do
this procedure? Should I have used anesthesia? Do
I need a dental license to do this? What would some
ambulance-chasing lawyer say? Would he accuse me
of wantonly and without regard for his smile, re-
moving Mr. Rangoon's teeth? What would Mr. Rangoon tell his family when he went home tonight?
"Honey, I went to the hospital and some young doctor took out my teeth." I was concerned. So I did
what all concerned young physicians do. I called a
consult. Not just a consult, a whole mess of consults.
Almost every consultant in the hospital had his
beeper go off. I wheeled Mr. Rangoon into the main
ER. He was covered with blood and speaking inco-
herently. I sent the eager residents to "work up the
new trauma." In minutes he was swarmed by white
coats. He had blood tests and urine tests, chest X
rays, EKGs, CT scans of the head and facial bones;
he was poked, prodded, pricked, swabbed, and
smeared. I did a little creative writing of my own,

mentioning that I had triaged a patient who reported being beat up outside the hospital, before he passed out from acute intoxication.

Several hours later, I was still disposing of the evidence, scattering teeth in trash cans and emesis basins all around the ER. A surgical intern asked me if I had seen the "bum" with the "really messed up face" in room 3. Naturally I told him "No," but did not give up the opportunity to remind him that "bum" is a pejorative appellation, and the preferred term is "economically challenged." Chastened, the intern reported that the "economically challenged" individual was supposed to be an eccentric carrying a shopping bag full of money when he was robbed and beaten mercilessly by some drug dealers just outside the hospital. "Really!" I exclaimed. The intern reported that Mr. Rangoon was admitted to the neuro intensive care unit to rule out cerebral trauma. I was impressed how the story had gotten so blown out of proportion, but did a quick scan of the ER for a shopping bag just in case. This place would keep a TV show in business for years.

Cathy and I are presently considering jobs in the big sandbox, aka Saudi Arabia. We are speaking to an oil company who needs doctors and nurses to take care of their employees while they are overseas. Our hope is to make enough in a year or two to pay off the student loans, and maybe have some left over for a down payment on a shack d'amore. We are flying out to Houston for an interview. They are putting us up in a nice hotel where we plan to start our towel-and-sheet collection, just in case the job doesn't pan out. I'll keep you abreast of any developments.

Warm regards,
Campion "Camel Jockey" Quinn

## IV

Dear Larry,

It started as a regular day at St. A's yesterday. The usual fun and games: drunks, crackheads, homeless, MIs, and lacerations (here they call them "lacs," as in alas and alack.) Just your garden variety stuff.

Late in the afternoon, the nursing-home crowd started showing up. One of them was an elderly Hispanic man, Mr. Ortiz. He came via ambulance from the Bailey-Slavin Nursing Home, known colloquially as the Barely-Livin' Nursing Home. He was sent over for dehydration and sepsis, a common enough problem in his peer group. Mr. Ortiz's chart gave his main diagnosis as "severely demented" (what a surprise) and said he was a "behavior problem." A cursory exam revealed a wasted man covered with urine and feces; bedsores gaped at his sacrum, and both his legs were red and swollen with infection. He exhibited an interesting neurological finding, a combination of echolalia and perseveration. When moving him during examinations, he shouted, *"DIOS MIO, DIOS MIO, DIOS MIO, DIOS MIO"* incessantly. After drawing blood he changed to, *"AYUDEME, AYUDEME, AYUDEME, AYUDEME, AYUDEME, AYUDEME . . ."* And . . . well, you get the idea. This shouting took on the character of Chinese water torture. Mr. Ortiz possessed a loud, clear, rather high-pitched voice, as older men sometimes do. It had a nails-on-the-chalkboard quality.

The *AYUDEME* doggerel continued for several hours. Tension was building. It became increasingly difficult to think or talk or do anything in a nice way with the constant shouting. Finally, I walked over to the stretcher, leaned in Mr. Ortiz's ear, and shouted "SHUT YOUR FACE!" He took this lapse of mine very well and was quiet for several seconds. The silence began to settle. Everyone in the ER seemed relieved, and I was halfway back to the counter when I heard, "SHUT YOUR FACE, SHUT YOUR FACE, SHUT YOUR FACE . . ." This got great yuks from the worker bees. It was not long before members of the staff had Mr. Ortiz repeating their favorite expressions: EAT ME, SHITHEAD, FUCK DOCTOR————(place the name of your favorite attending here), and the immortal FRANK BURNS EATS WORMS. Despite this feast of the intellect and flow of the soul, I was becoming unglued. It is very difficult to compose even a minor chart note while someone is shouting, "EAT ME, EAT ME, EAT ME . . ."

In the midst of all this din, Mr. Rios arrived. While smoking crack and drinking to excess, he had neglected to take his Dilantin. He was seizing with considerable vim and vigor, and these seizures were not responsive to my ministrations of Valium and magnesium. He eventually responded after I added a gram of phenytoin intravenously to the mixture. It was good that it worked, since he showed no signs of tiring. Mr. Rios was a stocky man whose arms were covered with homemade tattoos of snakes and skulls. His chin sported a goatee, and there was a livid scar under his right eye. Two earrings in his right ear and a "rattail" at the nape of his neck completed his fashion statement. All in all, he was the very flower of urban youth. He had no doubt lived a hard life. When he began to get agitated we gave him a little more Valium, for fear of him seizing again. He began to snore and slept peacefully, oblivious to Mr. O's vocalizations.

Several hours passed and Mr. Rios awoke suddenly and became quite demanding. He requested food, scotch, and "my fucking money." Since there were no bank tellers or barmaids immediately available, his requests went unheeded. This did not stop him from asking for it, though. His shouting went on and on, blending with "EAT ME, EAT ME, EAT ME . . ." The volume in the ER was becoming unbearable. Mr. Rios, no doubt an honors graduate of some assertiveness-training course, called out to whomever was in earshot for his food, scotch, and money. When they didn't comply he would castigate them in a ferocious manner. To a nurse, "You cunt! I'll fuck your daughters and strangle your infant sons!" To a transporter, "You faggot! You pussy! Come over here and suck my cock!" And on and on in this manner. I found it hard to relegate this to purely background noise. When Mr. Congeniality got up off his stretcher and shoved a nurse who was trying to quiet him, I was ready to do my all to shut him up. I was joined by several other members of the staff. We grabbed him and threw him onto the gurney. Our intention was to hold him there while a nurse drew up another dose of Valium to quiet him. (Although it is strictly against hospital policy to use "chemical restraints" on a patient just for the convenience of the staff.) This upset him to no end. He was mortally offended, as if we were old friends who had just betrayed him. Whatever decorum he had been observing was completely gone now. He sprang from the gurney, snarling, and tossed me into a wall. Dr. Bernstein and several other staff members entered the fray, Mr. Rios holding his own, kicking and biting anyone who came near him. I tackled him and forced him backward into a wheelchair. The security guards arrived with the leather restraints. I stood in front of the chair and pinned his arms to the chair's armrest. The guards tried to put on the restraints. Now Mr. Rios was looking directly into my face. He was struggling mightily, and was lifting me and the chair off the ground. I was terrified of his strength and what would happen if he got loose. I could smell his fetid breath as he cursed me, then he spat in my face. Just as I was thinking how disgusting this was, and how he probably had some lethal form of TB, he kicked me squarely in the testicles. I didn't think of much then at all. I was both trying to get away and yet not let go of his arms, very difficult indeed. He half stood from the chair and was trying to bite my nose when I butted his face with my forehead. He slumped down in the chair, a four-centimeter laceration across the bridge of his nose.

I retired to the washroom to rinse the sputum off my face. A lump was rising on my forehead, a pain was raging behind my eyes. I sat down in a back room to compose a note that looked favorably upon this occurrence. Even from the back room I could hear the strident voice of the intern trying to calm Mr. Rios enough to suture his laceration. Mr. Rios was winning this encounter. Mr. Ortiz was now echoing Mr. Rios's "FUCK YOU, FUCK YOU, FUCK YOU, FUCK YOU . . ."

Later in the evening, Mr. Rios took on a cop who was standing near. The cop was one of the many that keep an eye on patients that are handcuffed and in police custody. Mr. Rios continued in his usual MO—"Suck my cock," etc., etc. I sat behind the counter admiring how this cop could take such abuse without comment. He did not tell Mr. Rios to shut up or quiet down. He did not threaten him with arrest, or physical harm. His refusal to acknowledge the abuse only enraged Mr. Rios more. I wondered if they give the police a special course in this technique. Maybe he is so used to street crime and physical violence that this abuse does not bother him. Maybe he is deaf? I was feeling less of a man for overreacting to Mr. Rios's abuse. I was about to get up and offer the cop a cup of coffee when I noticed him looking from right to left, down the hall. He took two quick steps to the wheelchair, and when he thought no one was looking, gave Mr. Rios a left hook that snapped his head backward. He slumped in the wheelchair again, his right eye closing with a hematoma.

Two new injuries and a significant amount of Valium were not enough to chasten Mr. R. Within minutes he was awake and abusing staff members. Despite the fact that there were more tests pending, I discharged him onto the street, escorted by our biggest security guards, before someone put a bullet in his head. I wonder how this guy lived to be twenty-six-years old.

Mr. Ortiz was admitted upstairs. His final comments to the ER he had entertained for seven hours were, "BED 9 WINDOW, BED 9 WINDOW, BED 9 WINDOW," so we all knew the bed he was going to.

Cathy is pregnant. Suffice to say, I am pleased. Last week I went on an interview at TELOS Laboratory Associates, a pharmaceutical research firm. I listened a long time to their spiel, then told them I was morally opposed to human experimentation if I was paid only sixty-five thousand dolla a year. I can't believe I've even considered a research job! I hope your wee man is doing well and that you have not demented his mind with hospital stories.

Warm regards,
Campion

**V**

Dear Larry,
  Today I took care of a young professional couple.

They were minding their own business, watching a video in their swanky Village apartment, when a ring at the door announced a persistent solicitor. Mr. Smith opened the door and was smashed in the face with a gun butt. Two men entered the apartment, drew pistols, and threatened to kill the couple if they screamed. The assailants calmly and methodically ransacked the apartment, looking for money and valuables. Satisfied that they had everything they could carry in their bags, they turned their attention to the Smiths. Mr. Smith was beaten unmercifully, and with a gun to his head, his wife was forced to perform oral sex on the other perpetrator. Next she was raped and sodomized by both intruders as her husband watched. The Smiths were bound and gagged, as the burglars made several trips to empty the apartment. The couple was found by neighbors in the morning when their door was noted to be open, and they were brought to the ER.

Mrs. Smith had the vitreous look of those involved in major trauma. She spoke little, and then in monosyllables. She gave an eerily calm monotone description of the attack. Mr. Smith wasn't much better, with his facial-bone fractures and scalp lacerations. He didn't answer most questions, nor did he react when injected with tetanus toxoid or lidocaine when suturing his wounds.

I had a strange feeling of guilt while examining Mrs. Smith. The exam is intrusive. During the interview, the doctor is in charge of gathering information and evidence. One must ask all the unpleasant details of Who? . . . How many times? . . . How many attackers? . . . Orally? . . . Rectally? . . . The examination involves a pelvic and rectal exam. We are looking for trauma, semen, blood, and saliva. Hair samples are pulled from her head and pubic area; the pubic hair is combed for stray hairs of her as-

sailant, which may be matched with the assailant's
if he is caught. Bite wounds are swabbed for traces
of saliva, which also may be matched with the assailant's. The exam is a significant invasion of a patient who does not need any more stress. All during
the exam, Mrs. Smith was staring blankly into the
ceiling as I and two nurses discussed the wounds,
documented findings, bagged evidence. I was happy
to turn the case over to the rape-crisis counselor.
There was no counselor for Mr. Smith. He was sent
to the head and neck service for repair of his fractures. Mrs. Smith went home with her sister. As
usual, the police were all over the ER, hogging the
phones and writing space. I asked the sergeant what
the chances were of the assailants being caught. He
laughed and said something sarcastic about them
feeling guilty and turning themselves in later today.

I can only imagine the tremendous feeling of par-
anoia one must have after an incident like this,
knowing one's home is not safe. Wondering every
time someone rings the doorbell, Is this another rap-
ist, burglar, or worse?

This case really hit close to home. I've reminded
myself to add a deadbolt to our door at home, and
am thinking again about purchasing a handgun.
That couple had so much in common with us. I don't
know if I can tell Cathy about it. She's going off to
St. Thomas in the Virgin Islands to get some sun
with her sisters before the baby comes. Maybe when
she gets back I will.

Be safe,
Campion

**VI**

Dear Larry,
Yesterday morning when I left for work I felt like

I was getting the flu. I had slept poorly the night before and hoped for a calm day. It was not to be. The day was filled with the usual amount of inner-city nonsense. I became preoccupied with watching the clock and how slowly it seemed to move. I know it's a bad day when I start by saying, "Only eleven and a half hours to go!" The day dragged on without a chance to sit down or eat.

Needless to say, I was very happy when Patty Flanagan arrived to replace me. Patty and I went to medical school together. She's now a pulmonary fellow and works one or two nights a week to supplement her salary. She's an extremely bright, hard-working physician, and usually takes up all the slack in the ER when she's here. I was looking forward to a trip to the gym for a quick workout and a simmer in the Jacuzzi. While signing over cases on rounds I noted that Patty was quiet and appeared pale. I tried to ignore it, but when she left rounds to vomit in a wastebasket, it became difficult. Everyone was uncomfortably looking at one another, then down at their shoes. We all knew that the ER could not be left unmanned, but no one was interested in staying. Patty returned to rounds, said she was "OK," and we continued. When rounds were finished there was a general rush for the door by the attending staff. I was left with Patty, and in my medical opinion she looked like shit. I suggested that she take some Tylenol and Compazine and rest for a couple of hours while I covered things for her. I felt bad for her since she would have to be on duty the next day, sick and without any sleep, to work with the cancer patients. It seemed like that job was depressing enough without the added burden of being sick and exhausted.

The evening traffic was picking up and I was getting more weary. I had not eaten since morning. It

was now 10 P.M. and the Jacuzzi closed at eleven. I
decided to call it a night and went to look for Dr.
Flanagan. I found her lying on the floor of the coffee
room, looking even more pale and sweaty. I picked
her up, hoping against hope that she was practicing
an unusual form of meditation, but it was not to be.
She was febrile, very ill, and could barely move. I
toyed with the idea of having the patients come into
the coffee room and tell her their problems as she
lay on the floor, but I didn't think it would really
work. I was screwed.

I called my boss, Dr. Kleiner, looking for help. He
told me that he would make some inquiries to see
who was interested in coming in at midnight. I
thought of someone calling me at 11 P.M. to ask if I
wanted to work all night in the ER, and knew no
one would even pick up the phone at this hour. I
also knew Kleiner wasn't about to come in, but I
called him back at midnight anyway, just to let him
know how I was doing. He told me he was concerned, and that if I left the hospital unmanned I
would be liable for a patient abandonment suit. I
thanked him for his concern and assured him I
would call again at 3 A.M. to let him know how the
night was going.

The night turned hellish. I saw a young man come
into the main ER flanked by nurses from triage. He
was covered with blood—not all that unusual, but
triage nurses never come into the ER so I was concerned. I walked over to him and introduced myself.
He was holding his abdomen and in a very calm
voice stated that he had been robbed and stabbed. I
asked him if I could look at the wound, he released
his hand from his abdomen and his intestines fell to
his knees like a bloody apron. "I think we need the
trauma team!" someone yelled. In the trauma room
I started a few big lines, pushed in fluid, ordered

some O-negative blood, and put a wet dressing on his abdomen. When the trauma team arrived, the surgical residents looked at his wound, then grabbed the stretcher and ran for the OR with smiles on their faces. Ordinarily they hang around the sickest ER patients, asking for different X-ray views and clotting profiles while discussing how you are mismanaging the case. But when there is a true emergency, they really can hotfoot it to the OR. They love to operate. Mr. Intestines did well, according to an intern who scrubbed on the case. He said that despite the dramatic appearance of the wound, no vital organs had been violated. He sounded disappointed.

Right after that, a guy working the night shift in a print shop uptown tried to remove a loose bolt from one of the presses while the machine was on. His right hand was crushed from the mid-forearm downward. The hand, surgeons said, was not salvageable, and the ortho residents removed the crushed part in the OR. They sent him back to the ER for a tetanus shot and a dose of antibiotics and said he should be discharged. This seemed cruel. I think that if you lose a major body part, you are entitled to at least one night in the hospital. I couldn't reach his wife. She was working a night shift. I felt bad, the guy losing his hand and all, so I gave him some morphine and let him sleep in the already crowded ER. In his sleep, I noticed that he tried to scratch his scalp with the hand that was not there.

Around 3 A.M. a woman came in with a complaint of "pelvic pain." I noted on the chart that this twenty-eight-year-old white female listed "dentist" as her occupation. I made some introductory remarks about the field of dentistry, trying to break the ice before I invaded her body. She was an attractive blonde with short hair and round horn-rimmed glasses that gave her a studious, yuppie look. My soliloquy was interrupted by Miss Dentist requesting that she be examined by a female doctor. I took this as a warning sign, and shot a glance at the nurse in the room with me. ER litigation is filled with women reporting that doctors examined them in an improper fashion. Granted, they may not know what is proper, but this doesn't stop a lawsuit from ruining a reputation. I wanted to run out of the room and get someone else to see her. I quickly explained that I was one of four male doctors in the ER, but if she wanted another doctor she could wait a few hours to be seen in the GYN clinic. She replied she was much too uncomfortable to wait and would agree to be examined by me if the nurse left the room.

Now I was really frightened! No way! "State law says you have to have a chaperon for GYN exams, for your own protection," I stated with gravity. This was bullshit, but I thought it sounded convincing.

I left the room to have the nurse sound her out. After several minutes the nurse came out and pulled me to an area several yards from the door of the room. "She has something caught in her vagina," she said.

"Like what? A tampon? A condom? A diaphragm?"

"No, something out of the ordinary." She smiled.

"A vibrator? A Coke bottle? A billy club?" I offered.

"No," she insisted, "out of the ordinary."

I thought, This nurse must be losing touch with reality or has spent too much time in the ER. I was really too tired for guessing games. "I give up."

"A room deodorizer."

"A what?"

"You know, one of those mushroom-shaped

things that keep your living room from smelling like your cat. She's tried to get it out for two days, and now it's getting painful. She drove all the way from Jersey to avoid seeing anyone she knew. She's pretty embarrassed."

I knew better than to ask how the mushroom had gotten there; last year I had made the mistake of asking a young man how a teacup had found itself in his rectum. What followed was a long, totally startling story that I immediately regretted asking for. He told me he was painting the ceiling on a ladder, and fell onto a couch on which he had placed his cup and saucer. And well, you know, it just got stuck up there. Hmmm, let me picture this: You're painting the ceiling. Nude. On a ladder. Intermittently sipping tea. Yeah. I can see it.

I reentered the room. The dentist was crimson. I assumed my flattest affect. I really did feel sorry for her, and wanted this to be over for both of us. The deodorizer was removed easily with the help of a forceps. The floral design was still visible, but it was not emanating the "fragrant springtime bouquet" advertised on its side. It was placed in a sterile container and sent to pathology, as are all foreign objects removed from people's bodies. I thought of my former classmate, a pathology resident, who would be examining this specimen in the morning. I decided to give him something to think about and jotted a quick note on the pathology request form. "Mushroom found on routine vaginal exam. Suspect new vaginal flora. Could this have grown there?"

After the mushroom left the room, the dentist regained some of her composure and said she had a long ride back to Jersey. She said she wanted to pay in cash so her insurance company would not be notified. I told her to take it up with the registrar. She thanked me for my time and signed her discharge form, which suggested that she follow up with her private GYN and restrain herself from the future use of room deodorizers.

The night went on. It was 5 A.M. and I was near crying. I couldn't think clearly. I was drinking Coke by the liter, even though I had sworn off caffeine months before. It was a scary situation, like driving when you're very sleepy. You can't stop but you're afraid that if you don't you'll crash. Eight o'clock came murderously slow. The patient flow had become a trickle. I was using the old dodge of ordering tests that would take hours to complete in order to delay decision-making till the next shift. That way I could sign out the case in the morning to someone fresh.

When the troops did arrive, they seemed so awake and enthusiastic it made me sick. I was sullen during sign-out rounds, and explained in the fewest words possible events of the night before and conditions of the patients.

When leaving the hospital I was so relieved I actually felt refreshed during the walk to the train station, and thought it might be a good idea to read about abdominal trauma on the ride home. I fell asleep to the rhythmic clacking of the train, and awoke at the end of the line, an hour past my home.

Lately I've been moonlighting in an executive health clinic in downtown Manhattan. It is mostly people who want an excuse to go home and mistakenly think I will give it to them. When I'm working I take a personal interest in seeing that everyone else works too. I've so impressed the boss that he's offered to underpay me on a permanent basis.

Think I'll go back to bed,
Campion

## VII

Dear Larry,

This place is getting to be too much. Last week I was pulled from the ER to work on Unit Nine. This unit was conceived as an amenity to the ER and was marketed to local businesspeople as a place where they could receive prompt, courteous care by board-certified physicians for their sore throats and sprained ankles. The unit was painted in pastel colors and a few potted palm trees were purchased for ambiance. The marketing fell flat as the pressure in the main ER forced the less sick masses to overflow into the "corporate ER." As a result, captains of industry in thousand-dollar suits sat cheek by jowl with the homeless and unwashed. This put a speedy end to the whole corporate clientele, but the pastel and the palms remain. I think the street people really enjoy them—along with the *National Review* and yachting magazines.

I'd been tied up in the ER and by the time I arrived in the unit, there was an unruly crowd in the waiting room. They were backed up six to eight hours, due to the unusually large number of traumas resulting from a PLO demonstration/brawl the night before. Of course, my boss, Kleiner (the dyspeptic and dysfunctional graduate of a foreign medical school) decided to take me to task for my tardiness. I felt like I was back in school. I ignored him, which is how I usually deal with his inane comments, and went to work.

The only bright spot in the place was the preternaturally pleasant nurse Maria. She was quick on her feet, fun to talk with, and spoke Spanish fluently, all great assets in the ER. Maria told me that my first case was Mr. Sullivan. She mentioned that he was a denizen of Penn Station (i.e., homeless) and was "pissed off" because he had been waiting for six hours to see a doctor.

I entered the exam room and introduced myself to Mr. Sullivan, a forty-year-old white male with a medical history of alcohol abuse and ulcer disease. He said he had missed his clinic appointment and needed a drink, food, renewal of all his medications, and cab fare home to Penn Station. He further informed me that he had places to go and was not going to submit to an exam from some "snot-nose" young doctor. Being aware of the active black market for prescription medications, I told him the rules were "no physical, no meds." This did not have the desired effect. Mr. Sullivan became more aggressive and shouted that I was an "asswipe" and a "scumbag."

Usually, I'm pretty philosophical about these ad hominem attacks, even if they are *ab irato*. But cumulative events, combined with this morning's, had exhausted my equanimity, and I spoke some phrases *ab imo pectore* (in keeping with this sudden Latin bent of mine). I got in his face and told him in no uncertain terms, and in a loud voice, that he was a sodden drunk and an obnoxious motherfucker. I added that if he did not leave this ER immediately I, with righteousness in my heart, would smite him (i.e., knock his fucking teeth down his throat), thus rendering him *magnus mutas quam piscis* (quieter than a fish).

Mr. Sullivan evoked that classic Brooklyn comeback, "Go fuck yourself," and said he was not going to leave till I had given him what he came for. He waved his Patient's Rights Handbook in my face and told me he didn't have to leave if he didn't want to. I could feel my face getting red, and it was all I could do to keep myself from throttling him and throwing his body out on Seventh Avenue. He then threw himself on the floor and demanded to speak to his Patient's Rights Advocate, whom he mentioned by name. I could no longer control myself. I grabbed him by the collar and the seat of his pants and carried him to the waiting room, where I tossed him on the floor in the general direction of the exit. Now completely out of control, I screamed, "I'll kill you if I ever see you in this waiting room again."

A deathly silence fell on the usually lively waiting-room crowd. I looked into their faces, and for several long seconds not a word was spoken by anyone. Then I shouted into the assembled crowd, "NEXT!" No one came in for thirty minutes.

Stop by the hospital sometime and I'll meet you for dinner.

Vale, valeo,
Campion E. Quinn, M.D.

## VIII

Dear Larry,

3 A.M. Another attack of insomnia. The baby is well—she's hardly a baby anymore. Cathy and her sister are sleeping soundly. Maryanne is a frequent houseguest. She is a great cook, so we're always pleased when she comes to visit.

Yesterday morning was unpleasant. I spent it making phone calls to follow up the letters I mailed out several weeks ago to the biotech companies: fifty-three letters sent, fifty-two no's and one we'll-get-back-to-you, by a secretary. My ego is at an all-time low. My anxiety level is climbing in response. The following story will give you an idea of how things are going.

I was called into the office by Dr. Kleiner, director of the ER (I believe I've mentioned him before). He's a man with an unreasonably low opinion of me and quite an overinflated, undeserved opinion of himself. He's never worked in an ER before, but through political savvy and callow maggotry he wangled the directorship for himself. This has provided him with a salary, status, and virtually no responsibility. He has been able to maintain his internal medicine practice while his secretary handles all the ER administrative work. He is known as much for his lack of knowledge about the workings of the ER as he is for his inability to communicate with or to effectively manage the forty or so doctors for whom he is responsible.

With no preamble he informed me we were to make an appearance in the vice-president's office in response to a letter of complaint. The letter was received from a patient that I had treated for gonorrhea. He produced the letter, hand-written on yellow legal paper. It went thusly:

> "Dear Director of the ER:
>     I am writing to inform you of an occurrence which occurred at St. Alban's and has been detrimental to my life. I had the misfortune to come under the incompetent care of one of your doctors, C. Quinn. I had gone to the ER for treatment on May third . . ."

The letter went on to document his version of how he had come to the ER with complaints of a burning on urination and a dripping from his penis. I had told him he had gonorrhea and had treated him. I told him that he should tell all his sexual partners to come in and get checked. He told his fiancée, and then subsequently found out that the urethral cultures for gonorrhea were negative. This has led to much discord in his relationship with his new bride. This was all Dr. Quinn's fault.

What he failed to mention was that two days prior to his entering the ER he had been out with his friends celebrating his bachelor party. There had been strippers, who for a fee had engaged in sexual congress with him and his friends. This fun and games continued, with consumption of several "eight balls" of cocaine and much switching of partners, in what during the sixties was known as an orgy. The end result was that he had engaged in intercourse with four prostitutes in the same evening. This patient (let's call him Mr. Johnson) understood the significance of his symptoms, which is why he did not go to his regular doctor. What he did not realize is that he should not have had sex with his fiancée. He had hoped that he could have been treated and released, and never thought about it again. I told him that she was at risk for a serious pelvic infection that might make her sterile or kill her, and yet have no symptoms. This put Mr. Johnson in a real sweat. He asked me if I could tell her that he had contracted this infection while on Army Reserve training upstate from bad water or a tick bite. I refused, and thought that if she left him it would be the best thing for everyone involved. He left the ER with a prescription and a heavy conscience.

The urethral culture had sat on the desk of the ward clerk for twenty-four hours before going to the incubator, and therefore all the little gonorrhea germs in the culture tube had died off while waiting. It came as a surprise to no one that the results were negative. The results were sent to the patient, and this prompted much vilification of my name in the six-page letter. The castigation continued, calling for my resignation, suggesting removal of my license to practice medicine, etc. "How dare Dr. Quinn accuse me of having VD after only one chaste kiss from a cocktail hostess," he wrote.

After further castigation from the VP, who was not a physician by the way, I was told, "You are dealing with people's lives here, Dr. Quinn, and you should be more careful." He asked for no explanation and I was discharged from the office. Walking down the hall, I asked my boss why he hadn't backed me up in there with the VP. He gave me one of his pat answers. He has about three that he uses for all occasions. "Campion, when treating patients, remember that courtesy, competence, and caring are essential, and in that order." He followed up with number two: "Further, Campion, part of the job of emergency medicine is consuming a regular diet of humiliation that must be accepted for the benefit of the patients and the hospital."

Fresh from this, I was forced to call the fire department to assist in the removal of cock rings. Cock rings are devices that I've learned about since coming to St. Alban's. I suppose that anyone could use them, but here they are exclusively the province of the homosexual community. The rings are stainless steel and are placed at the base of the penis. They interfere with the blood exiting the veins of the penis, and so help maintain an erection. This can backfire and cause swelling that does not allow the cock rings to be removed. This is such a common problem that we have a schedule posted that tells us which days we can call the fire department or the police department to bring in the Whizzer Saw. It is a diamond-tipped saw that can cut through the steel rings. The patient reported abdominal pain and asked for a male doctor. I examined him. Whoa! His penis was swollen to the size and color of an eggplant. Violaceous, tender, and quite painful, he had hoped that ice packs and time would reduce the swelling. It had only gotten worse. He was not a

West Side "leather man" or anything. He had quite
a respectable job, and was very embarrassed. He
wanted me to cut them off so he could leave. I told
him that the three rings were quite a project and
would require the fire department to cut them off.
He moaned at the prospect. When the fire department did arrive, they all came off the truck, dressed
in the turnout coats, fire helmets, and smelling of
smoke. They were carrying the saw and associated
equipment. Apparently they do not share the physicians' sense of propriety, and laughed loud and
long when they entered the room. The patient's face
was as purple as his penis, but he just looked at the
wall and was quiet. The fire department was all
business after a few moments. They turned off all
the oxygen and set up a water line. The saw blade
and the rings would have to be irrigated to keep
them from burning his penis. When they started cut-
ting, a great plume of sparks flew from the rings. I
guess that's why they turned off the oxygen. The
patient shouted in fear but was restrained by the
burly firemen. The procedure took about ten
minutes. The firemen told him to be a good boy in
the future, and laughed as they carried their equipment out. The patient was asked to stay for urol-
ogical evaluation, but signed out against medical
advice. No guts, I guess.

Can I write myself a prescription for sleeping
pills?

Campion

## IX

Dear Larry,

I was pleased to hear from you. Has it really been
three years since you moved to the Midwest? We
have some catching up to do. Since I last wrote, I

quit St. Alban's, traveled Europe for six months, changed jobs three times, had another child (a boy), became a fellow in the American College of Physicians, and quit emergency medicine.

The first two job changes were to directorships of Emergency Departments. The staff of the first was very third world, with the most impressive credentials coming from Agra University. (You know, Agra, India, where the Taj Mahal is.)

The ER was very inner city, with all its attendant headaches and heartaches. I lasted six months and was involved in an equal opportunity discrimination suit. This stemmed from me firing a woman physician. She had released a young man with a "laceration to chest." He subsequently fell to the street a few blocks away and died. On autopsy he was noted to have had a serious wound inside his chest. The ER chart clearly demonstrated low blood pressure and difficulty breathing, but this doctor did not bother to examine him. She just sutured the wound like it was a mere razor cut to the finger and went back to sleep. This was gross negligence, and not an isolated incident of poor medical judgment. She was well known for missing diagnoses as well as work. She would conveniently get sick when she had night call, or have to go to her daughter's recital on her weekend shift. This caused much dissention amongst the ranks. So when this opportunity occurred, she was fired with the blessing of the hospital administration. She called a lawyer and a discrimination suit was filed. She claimed discrimination because she was a woman, a single mother, and an Indian (minority). What defense could we offer? She had only killed a patient. She was reinstated with back pay, and I (the discriminator) was encouraged to leave, so I did.

The next ER was in a well-heeled Long Island suburb. It was a busy place, but not like the city. The clientele included mink-coated dames with tennis elbows and injuries from riding their horses, along with older Wall Streeter types with failing hearts and livers. I lasted eighteen months. I was not as diplomatic as I could have been, and the nights were not getting any easier to do. Especially when there are children at home that won't let you sleep.

The hospital reorganized to accommodate health care reform. The leaner-meaner budget included a significant cut in ER expenditures for salaries and improvements in the physical plant. I saw the writing on the wall and updated my résumé.

I answered an ad in *The New York Times,* for a director of a medical department in a major Fortune 500 corporation. When I accepted the job, I had no idea of what I would be doing as an occupational medicine physician, but at this point I was willing to chance it. The salary was less than I had been making, but the lifestyle improvement is so significant that it makes it worth the change and more. I take care of the employees and executives. It's not challenging medicine, but I am home at 5 P.M., and no weekends. I'm sleeping through the night for the first time in ten years, and I love it!

I'll call you soon so we can make plans to get together.

Sincerely,
Campion

CAMPION E. QUINN, M.D.
*Rockville Center, New York*

# FRANK

As the ambulance-bay doors slammed open, Frank announced his arrival by shouting at the nurse, "Fuck you, cunt," punctuated at the end with the *phthoo* of phlegm being hocked at someone. I looked up from the patient I was treating and saw Frank rolling into the department, being held down on a gurney by two nurses, two policemen, and two paramedics. And they were struggling. Another nurse went to get the leather restraints.

"Let me go, you fucking cocksuckers!"

I excused myself from the bedside of the prim seventy-three-year-old Blue Hair. She had come in at midnight with the always dreaded complaint of "weak and dizzy for three months"—a syndrome that meant either her daughter wasn't paying enough attention to her or she was about to have a heart attack, and it was impossible to know which. Frank's language was not commonly heard in her living room. As I departed to deal with Frank, she was grinding her teeth quietly, eyelids fluttering, squeezing her complimentary copy of *Watchtower* with arthritic hands.

As Frank rolled in, he passed a four-year-old with a broken wrist waiting quietly in a chair next to his mother. Frank reared up on the gurney, made a monster face, and roared at him. The boy began to cry. Frank began to laugh.

"Fuck you fuck you fuck you," he shouted at the ceiling as he was rolled into his cubicle. Seven of us held him and applied the restraints that would pin his arms and legs to the gurney. He struggled and snarled and spit and snapped. We then stood back out of range to admire our handiwork.

"I'm going to sue you motherfuckers. I want your fucking names. I want everybody's name. I know my fucking rights." Then to one of the nurses: "What are you looking at, bitch? Huh? I'd like to fuck you in the ass." I stepped out of the cubicle to talk with the paramedics.

"What fine citizen did you angels of mercy bring to us tonight?"

"Frank here was out drinking and bullying people down at the Rebel Lounge bar and apparently used the word 'nigger' once too often in addressing another patron. They got into a fight and Frank got a knife in the back."

"Sorry it wasn't a gun."

"Well, we thought about stopping the ambulance and throwing him off the bridge, but we knew you were looking forward to seeing him."

"Where's the wound?"

"Down low, right side, back. Vitals are stable. Probably didn't get much."

"Too bad. Why is he in custody."

"He beat up one of the cops. He's on parole."

"What a surprise. Apparently his rehabilitation didn't take."

"Maybe next time."

"Our tax dollars at work."

I knew that he would need a CAT scan of his abdomen to see if the knife had cut into his kidney, ureter, or bowel. He would need to lie still for the scan and he would need an IV. I went back in to explain this to Frank. The room held that special odor created by bacteria growing in the warm sweat of the underarm for long periods of time. Frank was six feet, shirtless, and muscled. He had a goatee that tried to compensate for sparseness with length. On his left upper arm a tattoo read WHITE MAKES RIGHT in a crescent atop a swastika. On the other arm, two voluptuous women performed cunnilingus. He was deep in conversation with the security guard as I entered: "Your wife's home fucking a nigger right now, faggot." My presence in the room interrupted their little chat. His attention turned to me.

"Who the fuck are you, pussy?"

I felt the surge of adrenaline and the anger well up in my face. I stayed calm. "Frank, you have a stab wound in your back and we need to be sure it didn't cut anything life threatening. I need to start an IV and take some X rays of your stomach."

"Fuck you, cunt. You ain't doing shit to me. You touch me and I'll sue your fucking ass."

Jacked up on speed and booze, he felt pretty brave. But tomorrow morning, if he turned up sick or dead, lawyers would dance in licking their chops: "Our client's judgment was affected by the stress of his injury. You should have known that and treated him anyway." At trial, the lawyer would have him bathed, shaved, sheared, and suited, looking sad about his dead kidney and with all his illegitimate ragtag children assembled for the first time ever in a familylike pose in the front row of the courtroom.

I hated Frank and the parade of people like him

who increasingly inflict themselves on the Emergency Department, demanding we clean up after their latest self-indulgent mess.

"Frank, for your own safety, you need to let us get this test done."

"Make me, shitball," he taunted. He was beaming at me, very pleased with himself. He bucked his hips up off the gurney. "Come here, baby. Come here and suck my cock." At this time he managed to get his right foot loose and kicked one of the nurses hard in the chest. Security and two other nurses jumped in and restrained the leg. The kicked nurse was sore but OK.

"Ha! Ha! Ha!" he screamed at me. I was starting to get grumpy.

"Hold him down and start an IV and let's give him ten milligrams of Pavulon. Tell CAT scan to get ready. If he doesn't want to hold still for the scan, we can help him hold still."

Pavulon is a fascinating drug. It is most often used in surgery to completely relax the patient's body after he is put to sleep. It works by paralyzing all voluntary muscles. An awake person, when given this drug, cannot move a muscle, cannot breathe, open his eyes, swallow—nothing. Yet his brain is fine. He can think, hear, and feel everything. He is a totally alert prisoner in his own paralyzed body. His heart beats normally. A tube must be slipped into his airway and hooked to a ventilator to breathe for him. From the outside, he looks peacefully asleep. Inside, he is awake, helpless, and completely vulnerable.

Frank struggled against the IV, but without luck. The drug was injected and within a few moments the struggling and swearing slowed, then stopped. I slipped a tube into his airway and connected it to the ventilator. He looked peacefully asleep. But I knew better. I pulled up a chair next to his head so

I could speak gently into his ear.

I knew what I was about to do was politically incorrect. Frank no doubt had a mean mom, a drunken dad, and a cranky cellmate in prison. Therefore, his current "acting out" should be excused ad infinitum. But I was tired of him bullying the rest of us with his self-indulgent appetites. I wanted to frighten him. I wanted him to squirm.

"Frank, you've been a very unpleasant person tonight. You've been rude and vulgar and nasty and noisy. No one wants to put up with it. We are sick and tired of it. I don't see any way to avoid it. I'm going to have to castrate you. If anyone asks, we'll just explain that your balls and pecker were cut off in the fight. Who would disagree? I don't think you have many friends left here, Frank.

"We thought about just sending you down to the Patient Shredder and having you turned into fertilizer, but we were afraid it would kill the grass. So say good-bye to your genitals, Frank. No more hardons for you. But what a prize you'll make back in prison. You'll look almost like a woman. They'll be lining up to hump you in the butt. You'll be known as Frances instead of Frank. Frances the nutless wonder."

I stood up and put on two pairs of rubber gloves. With the big trauma scissors, I cut off his pants, then his underpants. His small penis lay slumped to the left. I picked up his testicles in my left hand and put the scissors close to his left ear and snipped them in the air. "Ready, Frances? It will only hurt for a while. Oh, and Frances, please try and hold still." I hefted his testicles in my left hand and air-snipped the scissors a few times. "Actually, Frances, I don't think these scissors will work. Let me go get the saw."

I left the cubicle, having finished torturing Frank,

and asked the tech to insert a Foley catheter in Frank's penis to check for blood before he went to the CAT scan. I hoped that the sensation of the tube being inserted would fool Frank into thinking he had been turned into a Frances. Soon after, Frank left for the CAT scan, catheter in place. Who knows what he thought.

The scan was negative. When Frank came back from the scanner, I whispered to him that he was going upstairs to a bed. "I'll be up to finish the job in a little while, Frances. Don't fall asleep." Frank was hospitalized overnight for observation. The Pavulon wore off and he was discharged back into police custody, to be rapidly recycled through prison and then unleashed yet again onto the community to continue his mission of misery.

I felt some guilt. I was sure that what I had done did not fall within the guidelines of the Hippocratic oath. But then again, Hippocrates probably didn't know Frank. I also had some fear of getting caught and ending up on the front page: DOCTOR TORTURES PARALYZED CITIZEN!

I felt some sadness. I went into medicine out of my affection for people and my hope to do them some good. My punishing Frank seemed like a betrayal of myself. But then I realized that Frank is the disease. The calm and reassurance I was able to create for old Blue Hair was wiped away in moments by Frank's savagery. She retreated then even further into her loneliness. Everywhere, people's lives are being poisoned by this new breed of savages who are forever protected by their "rights" and shepherded by packs of grubby lawyers braying and sniffing for money. When will it ever end?

RHODA GOODMAN, M.D.
*Washington, D.C.*

# P A R T
# NINE

Recently a three-year-old girl came in by ambulance from a car accident in which her dad and baby brother had been killed. Although she proved to have little wrong with her, she was crying because she was scratched and bumped and scared. We cleaned her up and her family came in to cuddle and soothe her. But she would, from time to time, begin to cry again softly, her inhale a series of tiny, quiet gasps. I thought about why she was crying. Although she couldn't really understand it, from this day on, for the rest of her life, her dad was gone. And no one, however hard they might try, would ever cherish her, hope for her, hold her, watch for her with the unending love that her dad would have held for her. I cried for her. I cried with her. I thought of my own family and I felt the intense preciousness and frailty of our tether to our lives.

The struggle against burnout is constant. After the jokes are told and the tricks are played, those that seem to survive best are those who recognize the *privilege of working in the wonderfully naked and powerful turbulence behind the doors, and those who look to see the grace in the face of what the doors bring in.*

# HARD RAIN

F our-thirty A.M., the darkest hour, too late to be
called night, too early to be called morning. The
hour when dreams become reality and reality is
dreamlike.

Inside the ER, I'm on duty. My eyes blink with
lids of thick sandpaper. The whites now are pink as
I rub to clear my vision. Hundreds of night shifts
and yet there's still no getting used to this blurry
feeling. The nurses know this. The smart ones take
the night shift for a few years, then go on to days as
soon as an opening appears. Night shifts wear on a
person slowly, relentlessly, almost seductively, rubbing away the protective armor of rational thought,
exposing the primitive self. Like fasting or meditat-
ing or doing drugs, the night shift is to be taken
seriously.

The hospital sleeps fitfully, narcotically, restlessly.
Inside, stark fluorescent lights hidden behind white
opalescent plastic panels create the illusion of day.
Outside, the wet blacktop holds pools of rainwater
reflecting the scarlet lamp from the ambulance now

gliding softly into the parking lot. The splash of tires
on wet pavement breaks the silence. The red light
casts a pulsating glow off the walls as the vehicle
backs under the overhang of the Emergency Department. The radio crackles with static. The doors
slip open with a pneumatic hiss. Warm antiseptic air
rushes out to meet the cold, damp night. The ambulance doors open, revealing a gurney inside holding a blanketed figure, strapped down, face up,
silent, motionless. The mouth opens and releases a
pained groan.

The call about the patient had come in a few
minutes before four. This night had not been much
different from most: A young woman needed
stitches, having cut her finger on the broccoli line at
Consolidated Canning; a couple of drunks had blood
alcohols drawn for the California Highway Patrol,
protesting their innocence in slurred, coarse voices—
voices that frightened a child needing antibiotics for
her ear infection. The ebb and flow of various stom-
achaches, backaches, headaches continued until 2
A.M.

I was ready to crash when the scanner called for
a paramedic unit at 4 A.M. "Man down near the
Clear Creek Bridge. Fire and police are on scene."
Damn! This is not what I want after being up all
night. The two night nurses share my lack of enthusiasm. Jenny sits on a stool near the radio filing her
nails. Mildred yawns. I go looking for coffee. As I'm
pouring, I hear the radio again. "Rockridge Base,
this is C-7, Code Two traffic."

Jenny's voice, "Go ahead C-7, this is MICN Duncan." I continue searching for sugar. "Hi, Duncan.
This is C-7. We're at Clear Creek Bridge. Police
found a fifty-year-old man on the sidewalk, unconscious. No ID, no name. He looks drunk but has a
cut on his head. He's waking up but can't remember

what happened. Vitals are stable. No other injuries.
We've got him in c-spine precautions. Any orders?"

"No, that's fine. What's your ETA?"

"We'll be there in five. The guy keeps talking
about his shoes, which is peculiar since he doesn't
have any. C-7 clear."

The exam room light is harsh, shadowless. The man
with no name and no shoes is strapped on the gurney, staring at the ceiling. His scalp is turbaned by
a large blood-soaked bandage. I make no move to
unstrap him yet, observing for a moment longer. His
rainsoaked clothes exude an odor of urine. He's
wearing a gray sweatshirt, loose and stained, with
FRESNO YMCA in faded letters. The sleeves are worn
through at the elbows, exposing bony arms. His
hands are callused yet delicate. His threadbare wool
pants are loose about his hips, the zipperless fly par-
tially closed with a safety pin. Bare feet, crusted with
mud, protrude from torn cuffs. His chest rises and
falls effortlessly. In fact, his entire body seems at
peace. Only his bloody face reflects his recent violence.

As I look, he speaks. "Look, Doc, they took my
shoes."

Startled by the sound of his voice, I step forward.
"What's your name? You know where you are?"

"Sure. Rockridge Hospital."

"Know how you got here?"

"Ambulance. Geez! Doc, my head really hurts!"

"Your neck hurt too?" I palpate his cervical spine.

"No, just my head. Hey, damn it! They took my
shoes. Those were good shoes—work boots from the
Goodwill. Hey, why do you got me strapped down
like this?" His eyes are scanning the room, his peace-
fulness replaced with agitation. "My name is Cal.

Cal Foster. Come on, Doc, let me get up. I'm all right."

"In a minute, OK? I want to look at that head wound first."

The nurses have come in while we are talking. Quickly, Jenny checks his blood pressure, pulse, and respiratory rate. I unwrap the dressings over his head as she finishes. The forehead wound is long and deep. I remove the straps. "So what happened?"

He talks, I probe. "Not sure, Doc. I've been drinking a little wine tonight, can you tell? Just staying dry under the bridge," he continues. "I was going to . . . Oh, shit! Now I remember. A couple of guys came up—wanted my bottle. I gave it to them—no trouble. One of these guys was really wild-eyed, fast talking—in Spanish. I didn't understand what he was saying. He started waving my bottle around. Hell, Doc! I moved out from under that bridge real quick-like, down toward the river—backing up— but him and his buddy just kept coming. Next thing I know there are cops around: My head hurts. I'm wet. I'm cold. My shoes are gone. . . .Hey! Can'tcha give me something for this headache?"

"All right, Cal, but I gotta sew you up."

"Go ahead, Doc. Don't wanna ruin my good looks." He lets out a wheezy laugh, hitting me with the fetid odor of stale cigarettes and cheap wine.

"Well, this is what I'm here for," I grouse to myself. I put on a mask. Cal and I are going to be close for awhile. I get my gloves and prepare the instruments as Mildred scrubs off dirt and blood, exposing the raw wound edges.

Cal closes his eyes and starts humming. I numb his forehead and begin my first stitch.

"Whatcha humming, Cal?"

"Oh, nothing."

"Sounds familiar." I keep sewing.

"Yeah? Well, it's from *Hair*. You look old enough to remember the sixties."

" 'Aquarius'—right?"

"Yeah, Doc. Did you know I was in that?"

"In *Hair*?"

"Yeah. In San Francisco. Small part. I was studying at the Actor's Workshop. Hell, I did directing, acting, set design, the whole thing. That's my career. Or was my career. I got off track a little."

"A little? I'd say you're way off now. What happened?"

"Sort of fried my brain, I guess. You see I was making ends meet by living with chicks, sort of a gigolo type. North Beach. Played a beatnik role. The older chicks dug it—letting me stay at their pads, then kicking me out. I'd go back to drinking wine and getting sandwiches at the mission—just keeping it together enough for a little work in the theater. Then I started doing methedrine, then acid, then ludes. Meth and ludes. Up and down. Moved to the Haight, became a hippie. Lotsa free love. Lotsa free everything . . ." his voice fades.

I'm still sewing. His wound extends from his forehead to far above his hairline. "I lived in the Haight in sixty-eight and sixty-nine," I tell him. "I used to eat lunch in Buena Vista Park once in a while."

"Hell, Doc, I buried my dog in Buena Vista Park." He opens his eyes and looks at me. "How much more you have to sew?"

"Not much," I reply, "but I have to shave your head a little to get to the wound up here. Maybe I should shave it all, kind of give you a Buddhist monk look."

His eyes widen further, fixing me with a penetrating look. "I am a Buddhist monk!"

"Come on, Cal . . ." I protest.

"Honest, Doc." He's not smiling. "I lived in Carmel Valley. Same retreat as Ira Sandperl, Joan Baez, the whole bunch of them. Shaved my head, wore robes, meditated . . ." his voice saddens. "Meditated myself right into the nut house and five years of Thorazine. Called me a paranoid schizophrenic."

"Are you?" My question is flat, nonthreatening. I return his gaze.

"Not anymore. The shrinks now say they were wrong. Now I'm a manic depressive—a lithium and Cogentin man. Actually, I'm doing a lot better."

"Sleeping under bridges? Rolled for wine and shoes?"

"Listen, Doc, I've got a girlfriend now. We've made plans. I think we'll do it. She and I both got disability checks. We're going back to the land. Maybe Mendocino." His eyes close again. I finish the last stitch and remove my gloves. Mildred begins cleaning the remaining blood from his forehead.

I turn back to Cal. "You can go when she's finished."

I look up at the clock. It's 5:30 A.M. and my back aches. My feet are sore. I'm definitely ready to call it quits for the night. I stretch and walk to the emergency room glass door. The rain has stopped and pale light is changing the sky in the east. I look down at my shoes. They're old but sturdy. Good for someone on his feet a lot, and Mendocino's a long way on foot. I return to Cal's room.

An hour and a half later, I slosh out the back door of the ER, headed for my car. The pavement is cold and wet under my bare toes. To me, it feels good. It's no longer night. It's morning.

KENT BENEDICT, M.D.
*Aptos, California*

# COMMUNICATING
# IN THE ER

Communication in the Emergency Department is a vague art, taught (ad nauseam) in school, mastered only in practice. Medical personnel can write an entire history and physical without using a single word, symbol, or initial recognizable to the average layperson. In the ER, it's not only what we write and say, it's what we really mean when we write or say it.

Picture an eleven-bed emergency room on a moderately busy afternoon. Mr. Patient in bed 5 has a lacerated arm. I am the trusty physician's assistant assigned to deal with bed 5, but as I survey the room, I notice there is no place for me to sit as I repair the laceration. I have been on my feet since early this morning and getting to sit down is one of my favorite reasons for repairing lacerations, so as I hastily assess Mr. Patient and move on to bed 6, I tell a nearby volunteer: "I need a stool in bed five."

Now, the volunteer is fairly new to the department, and eager to do a good job. She has not yet caught on to the standard reply to a request from a physician's assistant, which is usually "Get it yourself." But she has been exposed to the art of ER communication; she knows the SOB in bed 1 is not a bad person but "short of breath," and she knows "bed four needs a chest" is not a physique appraisal but an X-ray appraisal. So, when she hears my request, she approaches the treatment room nurse and says:

"The P.A. needs a stool in bed five."

The volunteer looks a little embarrassed. The nurse looks at me and asks: "You need a stool in five?"

I answer: "Yeah."

If communication is an art, we begin to create a masterpiece.

The nurse asks the nurse's aide to get a stool specimen container and instruct the patient in bed 5 while she makes the requisition.

The N.A. approaches bed 5. Mr. Patient is wearing a hospital gown. His laceration is not readily visible. The N.A. shows the specimen container to Mr. Patient and tells him he must provide a bowel movement in the little bowl. Mr. Patient tells her she must surely be mistaken, and refuses. What to do?

The nurse's aide approaches Dr. Hart. Dr. Hart is the supervising physician on duty. He does not know Mr. Patient in bed 5 from Adam, but he trusts his faithful physician's assistant. The N.A. tells him: "The patient in bed five won't give a stool specimen."

Dr. Hart gives sound advice: "If it is just for a stool culture, we can get by with a rectal swab. Check with the P.A."

The N.A. approaches me and says: "Can I get a culture swab on bed five?"

I am confused. I ask: "Who suggested a culture?"

She replies: "Dr. Hart."

Well, I was not aware that bed 5 needed a culture,

but I respect my omnipotent supervising physician. Perhaps he knows something about the patient that I missed. A weakened immune system? Contaminated wound? I decide I will investigate further before the specimen is sent to the lab. In the meantime, so as not to look foolish, I answer: "Sure, go ahead."

She goes to bed 5 with her culture swab. We can only imagine what transpires. What did not transpire was the obtaining of a rectal culture. She tells the treatment nurse: "Bed five is refusing his culture."

Refusing? She has been busy with other patients, but could it be that bed 5 was becoming a problem patient? (Now, everyone knows, once an ER nurse has labeled someone a problem patient, then that is what he is. Period. If you cross that bridge, buddy, there is no going back.) The treatment nurse, of course, knows the role of a physician's assistant. She approaches me and says: "Bed five is a problem. He is refusing his culture. You'll have to get it yourself."

Refusing his culture? A problem patient? What news is this? Did he read some *Reader's Digest* book titled *I Am Joe's Wound*? Some magazine article on how doctors are getting rich off of unnecessary lab tests? Well, I would speak to him. I approach Mr. Problem Patient.

"I understand you don't want your culture." I go on to wax poetically about the dangers of undiagnosed infections, the need to discover what type of bacteria he may be harboring, and the importance of cultures in general. I am getting nowhere. Mr. Problem Patient is adamant. And I'm not sure, but does he look a little confused? Apprehensive, maybe? Of course! Not to worry. I try another approach.

"Don't worry about any pain during the procedure. I will numb the area first with some Xylocaine." I then lay the syringe in full view on the counter and go in search of a stool on which to sit as I close the wound. Didn't I ask the volunteer to find me one?

As I culture, clean, and close the laceration, Mr. Problem Patient is very quiet. He has tucked the blanket tightly around his waist. He looks a little pale. I'm not surprised—many a strong man has gotten woozy at the sight of blood. When I finish putting on the dressing, he practically runs from the exam room.

As I dictate the note, I see there is a requisition for a stool culture clipped to the chart. The story unfolds.

Bed 5 never did return for his follow-up. Not surprising. After all, he was a problem patient.

RHONDA L. PERRY, P.A.
*Honolulu, Hawaii*

# DOWN THERE

The GYN nurse put another patient in the next available stirrups and called me. "A four-hundred-pound fourteen-year-old with severe, generalized abdominal pain. LMP now. Never sexually active," she informed me.

I went into the GYN room and introduced myself. The patient was extremely obese, sweaty, and screamed with pain intermittently. My first thought from about four feet from the GYN examining table was that the patient had a ruptured appendix.

The patient told me that she had been in pain for twelve hours, was nauseated, and had vomited. She had never been pregnant and had never been sexually active. Her menses had begun two years previously and had been irregular. The patient's mother, a woman of similar body size, told me that the patient had become irregular after gaining 150 pounds during the last eighteen months.

The patient's exam was not remarkable. The pain was in remission during my abdominal exam. The patient's gut was enormous and prevented an adequate abdominal exam. I ordered blood. While the blood was being drawn, I asked the patient in private if she had ever been sexually active. She said no. Furthermore, she said no one had ever touched her "down there," and she refused to have a pelvic exam.

I talked to the patient and to the patient's mother about the necessity of the exam. The nurse also talked to both of them. I returned in fifteen minutes. The patient's pain had increased. She writhed and screamed periodically, her pain now severe enough to persuade her to allow the pelvic.

I inserted the speculum into her vagina and saw a smooth, bloody, shiny mass covered with hair. She screamed and it shot out at me and into my lap, nearly sliding down my legs onto the floor. I wrangled the slippery mass back within my grasp. The mass wriggled. It screamed. I clamped and cut its umbilical cord. We broke open the emergency delivery bag and suctioned the eight pound baby. I placed the baby cautiously upon the mother's abdomen and held it there.

"Aaaaaah," she screamed. "That didn't come out of me!"

"That didn't come out of her!" yelled the mother.

"Well it certainly didn't come out of me," I said quickly, impulsively.

"I'm fixed. Hysterectomy," the nurse said.

We called the obstetrician, the pediatrician, and social services, then moved along to the next patient.

MICHAEL ERICKSEN, M.D.
Los Gatos, California

# KEEP ON SMILING

We receive many letters in the Emergency Department. Some express gratitude, others do not.

An elderly, female patient was brought to the emergency room and pronounced dead on arrival. Some weeks later, a letter arrived from her family thanking the ER personnel for the kindness shown to their aunt. The family was particularly appreciative that the staff had donated a set of false teeth, making the patient look especially beautiful at the wake. The letter also related how the deceased had always wanted to get false teeth but had been unable to afford such a purchase.

The hospital wrote back thanking the family for their kind remarks, but everyone remained perplexed by the comments about the teeth.

The mystery was solved with the receipt of another letter. This one was from a former patient complaining that she had been made to wait in the ER for three hours before being admitted to a hospital room. She was most disgruntled by the fact that the hospital had lost her false teeth and caused her a great deal of stress and inconvenience.

Thinking it best not to explain, the hospital sent a letter of apology and agreed to reimburse the cost of new dentures.

JOHN DENTE, M.D.
*Wilmington, Delaware*

# JUST BEING THOROUGH

Three men walked through the entrance door that was immediately beside the triage desk. Sharon, an excellent nurse, could tell at a glance the one in the middle was in trouble. He was being assisted by the men on each side. He had on a bicyclist outfit—jacket over tight, light blue shorts and bike shoes. He had one hand loosely over his groin, which was covered with blood. Sharon was told he had fallen.

She quickly got him onto a stretcher with his friends helping on either side. With rapid precision, she pulled down his shorts, removed the athletic supporter, spread his legs, and elevated his testicles, looking for the source of the bleeding. "What are you doing?" asked one of his friends.

"Trying to see where he's bleeding," she responded.

"It's my shoulder that's hurt," said the startled patient.

Under his waterproof jacket, the patient had a compound clavicle fracture that had bled down his chest and abdomen and covered his pants with blood. The hand that appeared to be protecting his groin was actually his injured arm being held by his other arm to protect it from movement.

The nurse won the award for the most thorough physical exam performed for a shoulder injury.

MARILYN J. GIFFORD, M.D.
*Colorado Springs, Colorado*

# BRIAN'S STORY

The ER day shift started out as usual, somewhat slow and under control. The staff was chatting about things going on with their home lives when the radio alarm went off. "AV Hospital, this is Hall Ambulance 242 with a pediatric full arrest." I handled the call, thinking, "Probably another SIDS baby." After twelve years as an ER nurse I know that not many of these kids survive. I thought of the parents and, as I was a new father, I felt especially bad.

I went outside to make sure the door was held open for the paramedics. My coworkers prepared the room for the patient. When the ambulance arrived, a paramedic came out of the back holding the child in one arm, doing compressions on the lifeless little body with the other.

As he hurried past me I looked at the child's face. A lump formed in my throat as I thought, He looks just like my baby. I realized this was the first dead baby I'd seen since my child was born. I followed the paramedics into the ER, dazed and dizzy. As I entered the room, one of the nurses looked at me and said, "Don't even come in here. We'll take care of this."

I mumbled, "Thanks," walked into the radio room, shut the door, and fought back the tears.

The child didn't survive. The parents arrived and were told of the outcome. Their screams and cries tore a hole right through me. I wanted to go to them, hug them, and cry with them, but I couldn't lose control of myself.

I fought my feelings hard, kept myself semicomposed, and yearned for my son. I wanted to see him and hold him. Now! The time passed slowly. I felt like I was in a different body. I spoke to my wife a couple of times over the phone throughout the rest of the day. I never mentioned to her what had happened for fear of losing control. She worries about our baby enough as it is.

The shift finally ended, and as I drove home, the knot in my throat began to disappear. I walked in the door, said hi to my wife, and gave her a kiss. I walked over to my son, Nathan. He was sleeping in his playpen. As I looked to make sure he was breathing, the tears welled up in my eyes again. I turned to look at my wife. She saw my face just as I said, "I had a SIDS baby today." We embraced, crying out loud, each other's necks wet with tears. I don't remember ever crying that hard in my life.

We calmed down a bit after about ten minutes, and I explained what had happened. I went to the sink to get a drink of water. The image of the lifeless baby came back. I thought of the parents and began crying again.

My son woke up and I held him close.

BRIAN COAKLEY, R.N.
*Lancaster, California*

# OPEN LETTER TO THE ER STAFF

There aren't many times that I hate to go to work, but Christmas is one of them. It's hard to be in the ER knowing that my family is home enjoying companionship, good food, and the joys of the holiday.

I was really feeling sorry for myself and quite resentful as I drove in to work following your plea for help. I'd already worked most of Christmas Eve, and had returned for a while on Christmas morning. And now you want me to come back Christmas night? But you'd sounded desperate, so I came.

Actually, I felt a little guilty. I thought back a few hours to Christmas morning and remembered noticing how you cheerfully greeted the patients as they streamed in. (Didn't they know what day it was?) I remembered noticing how you hid your own distress as you comforted the parents of the baby that had coded and died. I remembered noticing the caring support you gave on Christmas Eve to the husband and children of the woman dying of leukemia, not knowing if she would live through the night. I remembered noticing all these things and never complimenting you for them. By the time I arrived in the ER on Christmas night, my resentment was fading. The waiting room was crowded and the chart rack was full, but when I saw your tired faces and felt your welcome smiles, my resentment was gone. I slipped into my ER role and felt the energy that comes with true collaboration.

I suspect you wanted to be home as much as I did, but there wasn't any grumbling. We saw ninety patients that night. Most were sick, some weren't. For a few it was their last Christmas. The kitchen sent Styrofoam trays, holiday dinners for the staff, since no one could get away. When I finally left at 2 A.M., most of the trays were still sitting there, untouched.

I thought about us as I drove home. I thought of how we work together through the good and the bad, and of the experiences that bond us to each other. I realized that I had spent my Christmas with a great bunch of professionals I am proud to call friends. I realized how much you all mean to me and I just want to say thank you.

DAN CALIENDO, M.D.
*Wichita, Kansas*

# IN MEMORY OF J.W.

**8:07 A.M.:** A call comes in over the radio, "Code three." We are getting the victim of an auto-vs.-pedestrian accident, a seven-year-old girl. "Severe head trauma" is the description. Later we will find out that she had been dropped off at school by her car pool, had walked out between two cars to cross the street, and had been hit by the father of a classmate as he pulled up to drop off his own child.

The ETA is fifteen minutes. This patient will almost certainly need to be put on a ventilator. I scribble some orders on another chart, pull off my white coat, grab my stethoscope, and head for the resuscitation suite. I am the junior ER resident today, and my job is to take care of the patient from the neck up, including managing her airway. The senior resident will run the resuscitation, making management decisions.

**8:09:** I don a lead jacket to protect myself from all the X rays we'll be shooting, put on two pairs of gloves, and begin assembling all the equipment I think I'll need. I'm very nervous, because I haven't intubated many children and I'm not sure how big she is or what size endotracheal tube I'll need. I go through a formula in my head and grab a size 6 tube, with a 5.5 and a 6.5 for backup, placing them within easy reach on a Mayo stand. My hands are shaking. I insert a flexible metal stylet into the 6 tube to help guide it, and check the cuff balloon to be sure it inflates properly.

**8:12:** I am relieved to see the respiratory therapist arrive. She puts together a pediatric bag and mask to ventilate the patient by hand if necessary while we are getting ready to intubate. I hook up the suction, check to make sure it's working, and stuff the tip under the gurney mattress, where I can easily reach it.

**8:14:** I am rummaging through the drawers, looking for the right size laryngoscope blade to fit in this patient's mouth, so I can see her vocal cords when I intubate her. Finally I settle on a Miller 2, attach it to a handle, and make sure the light works. A Macintosh is also out and ready as a backup. The senior resident walks in, looking very cool, and puts on some lead.

"Have you called pharmacy?" he asks the nurse in charge.

"They're on their way."

"Why don't you draw up some etomidate, sux, and atropine. We'll figure out the doses."

**8:18:** I'm ready. I think.

**8:21:** The pharmacist, trauma surgeons, and neurosurgeon have all arrived. We all lounge around the doorway, looking down the hall for the paramedics.

**8:22:** "Rescue Twenty-eight in the parking lot with a code three," blurts the loudspeaker. I run to my spot at the head of the gurney and double-check all my equipment. My palms are sweating.

**8:23:** The paramedics wheel their gurney into the room, talking as they come and holding IV bags up in the air.

"She needs to be intubated," I hear one of them say. And indeed it is true. The child is breathing on her own, but her breathing sounds gasping and ragged. Each time she exhales she moans, an eerie, high-pitched moan, like a hurt animal; the same with each breath. She is unresponsive to stimuli. We transfer her to our gurney and everyone gathers around in the intimate frenzy of accomplishing our individual tasks. The X-ray techs are pushing people out of the way to get a chest X ray, while the trauma techs strip off her clothes, the surgeons feel her belly, and the nurses try to start additional IVs. The respiratory tech places oxygen on her to get as much as possible into her lungs before intubation. The pharmacist and the senior resident have agreed on the doses of medicines needed to sedate and paralyze her so that I can intubate her, and they signal a nurse to begin injecting the drugs.

I don't have much time. My heart is racing. I check her pupils: fixed and dilated. I look in her ears: no blood. I feel her bloody head for hematomas and instantly get a sickening feeling in the pit of my stomach—her entire skull is unstable. Even the slightest pressure on part of it results in clicking bone fragments and the squish of soft tissue against my other hand on the opposite side. Her left cheek is swollen and purple; there is probably a facial fracture as well. I call out my findings.

**8:25:** The drugs are beginning to work. The child gradually becomes flaccid, her teeth unclench, and she stops breathing. The cervical collar has been opened in front, and the respiratory tech puts pressure on the child's cricoid cartilage in her throat to keep the esophagus closed, preventing stomach contents from refluxing into her airway. The senior resident stabilizes her head for me, and I open her mouth and insert the laryngoscope.

My first view is of blood and saliva; I can't see anything that I need to see. Adrenaline and terror surge through my body. "Suction!"

Someone hands it to me, and the blood swooshes up into the plastic tube. I push the laryngoscope in a bit further and finally see the diamond of her little white vocal cords, like broken toothpicks guarding the blackness of her trachea.

"Tube!" Again it is handed to me, and I guide it into her trachea, never once taking my eyes off those vocal cords. "It's in!"

My left hand is clutching the tube at her lips for dear life. I pull the stylet out of the tube. The tech attaches a bag and begins hyperventilating the patient to reduce the swelling in her brain. The senior resident listens for breath sounds in the chest to confirm that the tube is in the right place.

**8:35:** The tube has been secured with tape and the child is hooked up to a ventilator. O-negative blood has arrived and is hung. A catheter has been placed in the child's urethra to drain her bladder. I snake an orogastric tube into her mouth, past the endotracheal tube and into her esophagus to empty out her stomach. The surgeons are worried, because the child's belly is firm and slightly distended. The neurosurgeon would like to get a CT scan of her head, but the trauma surgeons suspect they'll have to explore her belly in the operating room first. They are arguing politely. The senior resident is looking at X rays of the chest, pelvis, and cervical spine as they come out of the developer.

**8:42:** A second hematocrit comes back significantly lower than the first. Even though the patient's blood pressure is stable, everyone agrees she must be bleeding into her belly and needs to go to the OR. We begin "packaging" her—transferring the IV bags, monitors, oxygen, etc. to the gurney for transport.

**8:50:** The patient is wheeled out of the room with the surgeons at her side, leaving miscellaneous trash in her wake. The floor is strewn with needle caps, IV bag wrappers, gauze pads, and small pools of blood.

**8:51:** I go see a new patient.

**10:23:** The charge nurse has heard through the grapevine that the child had a double operation: The surgeons opened her belly while the neurosurgeons put a tube into the ventricles of her brain to relieve the pressure there. When they got chunks of brain matter back through the tubes instead of clear cerebrospinal fluid, they knew her brain was hopelessly damaged. The surgeons closed her belly back up without trying to find the bleeding site. The parents saw her for the first time in the recovery room and agreed to have her removed from life support.

**11:45:** I am writing up another patient's chart when I find a loose computer label with the child's name on it lying on the counter. Under her name is a ten-digit hospital number and her birth date.

My eyes fill with tears and my throat begins to burn. I go to the computer room to make an entry into the procedure log.

**11:50:** When I come out five minutes later, I am more composed.

VALERIE NORTON, M.D.
*Los Angeles, California*

# MULTITRAUMA

I know you are coming.
The voice over the airways warns me.
A voice which shares so much more
than facts and vital signs
(it tries not to).

Panic, fear, anger, frustration
overpower the static
and tear across the miles to my ears.
You are coming, the voice says,
and you are dying.

Preparation by rote.
Multitrauma coming.
Open fractures, sucking chest wound,
bad head.
Pedestrian, kid on a bike, no helmet.
Hit head-on by a car.

How old?
Maybe ten or eleven.
Force out the image that forms.
How far out?
Five minutes, no more.
I stand and wait quietly among assembled col-
leagues
and glistening instruments of resuscitation.
Arms folded, head slightly bowed,
eyes focused on the gray tiled floor.
I experience a strange detachment
from the activity taking place around me.

The trauma team.
Nurses focus on readying infusion sets and cutdown trays.
Technicians discuss the never-ending business
of their day.
Residents, looking dog-tired,
gown up in silence, pulling on gloves and ad-
justing goggles.
Medical students and junior residents,
wanting to appear in control,
are betrayed by body language
and pressured whispers.
Their affected indifference only emphasizes
their not so hidden emotions.
I am moved by this assemblage.
But I fear that no matter how well prepared,
we will not be able to save you.

"Patient in the trauma room."
The matter-of-fact, unemotional overhead

speaker voice
announces your arrival.
Worse than expected.
Intubated, CPR in progress.
Long board, collar, sandbags, two lines running.
Well packaged.
Paramedics sweat from their efforts,
their eyes and voices telegraphing
their disappointment and stress.

The ABCs of trauma care are welcome friends.
I immerse myself in the ritual
of this incredible process.
Protect the spine.
Secure the airway.
Central lines.
O-negative blood stat.
Crystalloid challenge through fluid warmers.
Emergent thoracotomy.
Cross-clamp the aorta.
Open-chest cardiac compressions.
We perform your last rites
in our way.

When it is over
and there are no more tasks to perform,
no more traditions to uphold,
no more heroics to attempt,
your humanness
and the tragedy of your death
force their way back into my thoughts.

For the first time I see you,
not as another victim of blunt vehicular trauma,
but as a child.
Fine features.
Sun-bleached hair.
The smooth, unblemished skin of youth.
Lean, muscular, an athlete's build.
Two colorful braided friendship bracelets
tied about your left wrist.
A handsome boy.

We quietly and gently clean your body
and prepare the room,
absorbed in our own thoughts of
personal mourning.
Your parents are nearby
expecting news of a miracle.
I am unable to comprehend the devastation
my visit will bring them.
I will share my own sorrow,
offer an embrace of understanding,
and be there to answer questions of Why?
and assuage guilt.

As I cross the hall to the grieving room,
I am again awed by the profundity
of this very precious responsibility:
bringing the message
of sudden and tragic loss
to those who must carry on.

I count myself among the survivors,
forever changed in some immeasurable way
by each untimely death I witness.
So much injury to the flesh.
So much injury to the spirit.
Multitrauma.

GEORGE L. HIGGINS III, M.D.
*Cape Elizabeth, Maine*

# EPILOGUE

*I looked at the doors today. They were quiet, closed. Resting. Waiting.*

*Earlier this morning they had brought in a ninety-two-year-old man. As he lay on the gurney, looking up at the ceiling in the glare of the treatment room, it suddenly occurred to me that someday this would be my son. My father would be a slight memory to him. I myself would be long dead. There would be grandchildren he'd played with that I knew nothing about.*

*The doors will have brought him in on this final occasion to the people inside. What will they know of him, those people caring for him on that distant day? Will they see in that old man's face any of the young boy that I look at now? Will they know that he was once wildly cherished and that every single day he was in someone's most tender thoughts?*

*They won't know that. And he won't need them to know that. What will he need, I wondered?*

*Just their kind presence.*

# THE VOCABULARY OF THE ER

The following is a collection of words used in the emergency room. Some are simply medical terms that appear in the stories and might be helpful to have defined. But they are interwoven with the slang of emergency medicine—words and phrases that do not appear in the text or in any medical text whatsoever. The slang is included for your information and perhaps your amusement. Some of the language may seem degrading if not outright nasty. In that respect it reflects the ongoing process of using humor or sarcasm to blunt the emotional impact of working in the Pit.

AGONAL: Just before or accompanying death, as in: "The heart was in an AGONAL rhythm."
AMBU BAG: Device used to ventilate a patient who is not breathing. *See* BAG.
ANEURYSM: An abnormal and dangerous ballooning out of a vessel, especially an artery.
ARREST: *See* CARDIAC ARREST.
ARTERIAL LINE: An IV inserted into an artery rather than a vein for the purpose of continuous monitoring of blood pressure.
ASYSTOLIC: Without a heartbeat. *See* FULL ARREST.
ATTENDINGS: Full-fledged doctors who, after training, teach in Emergency Departments that train new

doctors. (Often referred to as "offendings" by the HOUSE STAFF.)

BAG: To ventilate a patient with an AMBU BAG.

BLADE: A nickname for a surgeon. Surgeons are known to be bold and arrogant—often wrong but never in doubt.

BLEEDING ALWAYS STOPS: Need we say more?

BOXED: Put in a pine box (i.e., died).

BUG JUICE: Intravenous antibiotics.

C-SPINE: The cervical spine (the neck bones).

CARDIAC ARREST: When a heart stops pumping—i.e., the patient has dropped dead. Also ARREST; FULL ARREST. *See also* CODE; CODE BLUE.

CAROTID ARTERIES: The two big arteries supplying blood to the brain.

CAT SCAN: Computerized axial tomography. A fancy X ray that shows the inside of the body. Also CT SCAN.

CHANDELIER SIGN: In the diagnosis of PID during the pelvic exam movement of the cervix produces pain so severe that the patient has to be scraped off the chandelier.

CHARTOMEGALY: From "chart," referring to the medical record, and "megaly," meaning large or exaggerated in size. Refers to the chart of a patient who comes to the hospital very frequently or is a FREQUENT FLYER.

CHF: Congestive heart failure. When a heart gets weak and sick, it can't pump blood very well, hence the blood does not circulate well and the blood pressure drops. In addition, the blood returning from the lungs to the weak heart tends to back up into the lungs, making the patient very short of breath. When the blood pressure drops and the lungs fill up with fluid, the patient is called SICK. Expect a CODE BLUE.

CODE: To go into CARDIAC ARREST.

CODE BLUE: Announced with a specific location, it

means someone has gone into CARDIAC ARREST and needs resuscitation STAT.

CPR: Cardiopulmonary resuscitation—the practice of squashing dead people's chests in hopes of squeezing enough blood to the brain to keep them alive for a few more minutes until help arrives.

CRACK THE CHEST: To open the chest in order to stop massive bleeding or perform open-heart massage. *See* THORACOTOMY.

CRASH: When a SICK patient turns bad and starts to die. *See* DUMP.

CROCK: A malingering patient with bogus complaints, as in, "Every time the train goes by, my feet get numb." Order a STAT PORCELAIN LEVEL.

CT: *See* CAT SCAN.

CTD: Circling The Drain. A very SICK patient not doing very well. *See also* FTD; PBAB; STBD.

CUTDOWN: When it is impossible to successfully stick an IV through the skin and into the vein, it becomes necessary to cut open the skin and dig down to the vein.

DASH FOR CASH: Helicopter transport of critically ill patients. These helicopters are often owned and run by private companies that charge big bucks.

DEFIBRILLATION: Using a machine to shock a heart that is quivering (not beating) in order to try to normalize the heart's electrical activity into a regular beat again. Also SHOCK.

DFO: Done Fell Out (passed out).

DOA: Dead On Arrival.

DSB: Drug-Seeking Behavior—used to describe patients who come in with bogus complaints seeking narcotics in order to dull an otherwise unhappy life.

DUMP: This word has several meanings: 1) When a nursing home, a community physician, or another hospital DUMPS a SICK patient, (usually NEGATIVE WALLET BIOPSY) on the ER to be cleaned up and cared for. 2) When a SICK patient goes bad, he DUMPS or CRASHES. 3) As a noun: "The GOMER was DUMP."

DWINDLES, THE: Failure to thrive, especially in a GOMER.

ECHOLALIA: The repetition of words spoken by others, as if echoing them (associated with mental illness).

ECTOPIC PREGNANCY: The implantation of a fertilized egg somewhere in the body besides the uterus. Most commonly this abnormal location is the Fallopian tube; therefore it may also be called a tubal pregnancy. Ectopic pregnancies can rupture and cause life-threatening bleeding into the abdomen.

EKG: Electrocardiogram—a tracing of the heart's electrical activity.

EMESIS: Vomiting.

EMT: Emergency medical technician—a paramedic or an ambulance driver.

EPI: Epinephrine, or Adrenalin—a drug used to help restart the heart.

ET: Endotracheal tube; the plastic tube passed into the trachea (windpipe) when a patient is INTUBATED.

ETA: Estimated time of arrival.

FAMILY PLAN: One of the kids has a cold so the parents pack the whole family into the station wagon and bring them along to the ER "to be checked." Often used in association with the MAGIC KINGDOM CARD.

FEATHER COUNT: A measure of flakiness.

FELLOW: A doctor in subspecialty training beyond residency.

FEMORAL ARTERIES: The big arteries of the upper leg.

FLAIL: A resuscitation that goes badly.

FLATLINE: When the heart-monitor tracing no longer shows heart blips but only a flatline tracing reflecting the absence of heartbeat. *See also* ASYSTOLIC; CARDIAC ARREST.

FLEA: An internist, particularly one who orders multiple test results to establish a list of multiple possible diseases so that multiple further tests can be done, thereby sucking a lot of blood from the patient with no discernable benefit.

FLOG: A resuscitation on a patient who is essentially dead upon arrival to the emergency room.

FLUORESCENT LIGHT THERAPY: This treatment is reserved for those patients whose unpleasant manner has offended the triage nurse, who makes the patient sit forever in the waiting room, basking in the harsh fluorescent light.

FOLEY CATHETER: A rubber tube put into the bladder through the urethra to assure the flow of urine.

FOS: Full Of Shit—a severely constipated patient with abdominal pain.

FREQUENT FLYER: A regular ER visitor who comes in for drugs, minor problems, or social contact.

FTD: Fixin' To Die.

FULL ARREST: *See* CARDIAC ARREST.

GI: Gastrointestinal, or pertaining to the gut.

GOK: God Only Knows. Used to refer to a puzzling set of symptoms.

GOMER: Originally proposed by Dr. Samuel Shem to be a mnemonic meaning Get Out of My Emergency Room, but more generally used to refer to any debilitated, senile, elderly person. Also GOMED-OUT; GOMERTOSE.

GOMERGRAM: Since the gomer by definition can't describe her symptoms due to senility, a shotgun approach is used and every screening lab is ordered: EKG, CXR, CBC, Chem 7, UA, ABG, PT/PTT, LFT. This ordering of all possible tests is called a GOMERGRAM.

GOOMBAH: A worrisome mass or tumor found on exam or X ray. For example, one might say after reviewing a patient's head CAT scan: "He has a mean-looking GOOMBAH in the brain."

GORK: A patient who has sustained a brain injury resulting in severe mental impairment. One might say: "The patient is now a GORK (or GORKED OUT)."

HEMATOMA: A blood-filled lump that forms after trauma; a "goose egg."

HOUSE STAFF: INTERNS and RESIDENTS at a teaching hospital.

HYPOTENSION: Abnormally low blood pressure.

HYPOTHERMIA: Abnormally low temperature.

ICU: Intensive care unit. Also known as the "expensive care unit." (Often the last stop on the way to the "eternal care unit.")

INTERN: A young doctor in the first year of training after medical school (100-hour work weeks).

INTUBATE: To insert a plastic tube through the mouth (sometimes the nose) and into the trachea (windpipe) to help ventilate a patient.

IV: Used to administer solutions intravenously (in the vein).

LABS: Tests commonly used in evaluating a patient:
  CBC: Complete blood count of red and white blood cells.
  LYTES: Electrolyte levels.
  UA: Urine analysis.
  ABG: Arterial blood gas; checks the oxygen in the blood.
  CHEM 7: More blood chemistry.
  EKG: Electrocardiogram; measures the heart's electrical activity.
  CXR: Chest X ray.
  PT/PTT: Blood coagulation measurements.
  LFT: Liver function test.

LARYNGOSCOPE: A metal blade used to push the tongue aside and lift up the throat so that the windpipe can be seen.

LINE: An IV line for access to circulating blood.

LINE 'EM UP: To insert multiple lines in order to resuscitate and monitor a critically ill patient.

LMP: Last menstrual period.

LOL NAD: Little Old Lady, No Acute Distress. May or may not be a GOMER.

LP (LUMBAR PUNCTURE): *See* SPINAL TAP.

MAGIC KINGDOM CARD: A Medicaid card with monthly stickers. When an amusement park admission is free, the customer tends to come more often. Also known as "McStickers."

MI: Myocardial infarction—aka heart attack or "the big one," as in, "Oh shit, he's having the big one."

MICRODECKIA: "Micro" meaning small, "deck" as in a deck of cards—hence, playing with less than a full deck: "The patient is suffering from MICRODECKIA."

MONITOR: A cardiac monitor that displays the patient's heart rhythm.

NEGATIVE WALLET BIOPSY: Cash patient without funds. Also known as a no-cash patient.

NEONATE: An infant less than a month old.

NEURO: Relating to the neurological system (the brain and nerves).

NO CODE: A classification of a patient (with the patient's and family's approval) that if the patient should go into cardiac arrest, no effort should be made to resuscitate him.

NSR: Normal sinus rhythm—the normal pacemaker beating of the heart.

OB/GYN: Obstetrics and gynecology.

OR: Operating room.

ORTHO: Orthopedic surgery—practiced by bone doctors. In medical school the folklore reported that the bottom 10 percent of the class would be pithed (have their little brains destroyed by a sharp instrument). Those that could crawl away went into OB/GYN. Those that couldn't went into ORTHO. Hence the phrase "An orthopedic surgeon must be as strong as an ox, and twice as smart."

OTDMF: Out The Door, Mother Fucker.

OXIMETRY: A monitor of the effectiveness of a patient's breathing.

PATH: Pathology—that specialty of medicine that examines tissues and dead people to determine the nature of the disease or the cause of death.

PATHOLOGIST: A doctor who prefers the company of dead people and enjoys the smell of formaldehyde.

PBAB: Pine Box At Bedside—a suggestion for patients who aren't doing very well and are SICK.

PERSEVERATION: Persistent repetition of an action or words.

PHYSICIAN'S ASSISTANT: A licensed health care provider who does medical care under the supervision of a physician. Usually called a P.A.

PID: Pelvic inflammatory disease—a venereal gynocological infection.

PIT: Frequently used to refer to the emergency room by the people who work in it.

PLAYER: A patient.

POP DROP: When a family drops their elderly, disabled, burdensome dad off at the emergency room so they can take a vacation. *See also* POSITIVE TAILLIGHT SIGN.

PORCELAIN LEVEL: A term that stems from porcelain crockery, or a "crock," as in "a crock of shit." This is a fictitious blood test ordered at the bedside to communicate to a coworker that you think the patient is malingering and hence a DSB or TERRASPHERE.

POS: Pre-Orgasmic Syndrome—the male equivalent of PMS. Also known as "Irritable Male Syndrome."

POSITIVE SUITCASE SIGN: Noted about a patient who arrives in the Emergency Department with a packed suitcase. Generally denotes a diagnosis of "Needs a place to stay."

POSITIVE TAILLIGHT SIGN: Noted when a patient is

dropped off at the emergency room by the family and all we see are rapidly fading taillights as the family sedan speeds off into the night. Generally denotes a diagnosis of "Find him a place to stay." *See also* POP DROP.

POST: A postmortem, or autopsy.

PREEMIE: A prematurely born infant.

PRETERMINAL: Almost terminal, or nearly dead. *See also* CTD; STBD.

PULMONARY EDEMA: Fluid in the lungs, most often occurring with CHF.

PULMONARY EMBOLUS: A blood clot that forms in the body, breaks off, and travels to a lung, where it lodges, causing pain, shortness of breath, and, if it is big enough, death. Also referred to as a PE.

PVC: Premature ventricular contraction—an abnormal heartbeat that may warn of impending VFIB or VTACH.

Q SIGN: Usually found in debilitated patients (e.g., a GOMER) who are GORKED OUT. The mouth has slacked open into an *O* and the tongue hangs out to one side, forming a *Q*.

RAY: A radiologist—i.e., a person who likes to work in the dark but not make any decisions. Radiologist's national flower: the Hedge.

RESIDENT: A HOUSE STAFF doctor; still in training, but beyond INTERN.

RINGERS: An IV fluid used in resuscitation.

ROCK GARDEN: When the emergency room fills up with ROCKS.

ROCKS: Patients who can't be moved out of the emergency room. Often a GOMER, the patient is not sick enough to put in the hospital, but the family refuses to take him home. Sometimes, however, it can be a patient with a NEGATIVE WALLET BIOPSY, and no staff physician will admit him and no other hospital will take him in transfer. The worst possible rock is known as a "diamond."

ROUNDING UP THE USUAL SUSPECTS: Ordering all the tests and studies that routinely get ordered on a given type of patient. May often coincide with a GOMERGRAM.

ROUNDS: Usually occur at shift changes; the departing doctors and the newly arriving doctors go from patient to patient giving an update on each patient's condition.

SACRAL: Relating to the sacrum, which is the back wall of the pelvis (the tailbone).

SCUT: The lowest form of HOUSE STAFF work—drawing blood, labeling tubes, carrying labs, pushing patients to X ray, etc.

SCUT MONKEY: A medical student; one who performs scut.

SHOCK: *See* DEFIBRILLATION.

SICK: Sick. Real sick. May be CTD. Expect a CODE BLUE.

SIDS: Sudden infant death syndrome. Babies in the first few months of life suddenly die while napping. The reason is unknown but sometimes is associated with sleeping on the stomach.

SNOW: To give a patient high doses of morphine or Demerol when he is in a lot of pain.

SPINAL TAP: Insertion of a needle between the lumbar vertebrae into the spinal canal to withdraw spinal fluid in order to check for infection or bleeding. Also LP (LUMBAR PUNCTURE).

SPOTAS: People who come to the ER in hopes of obtaining a written excuse for not doing whatever it was that they were "spota" be doing: "I spota be in court right now, but every time the train goes by, my feet get numb."

STAT: At once; immediately.

STBD: Soon To Be Dead. *See also* CTD, FTD, PBAB.

STERNOTOMY: A procedure in which the chest is cut open through the sternum. *See* CRACK THE CHEST.

STOOL MAGNET: An unlucky medical student who gets dumped on with the worst scut and the nastiest patients.

TATTOO-TO-TOOTH RATIO: A prognostic indicator of a patient's self-destructive potiential.

TOURON: A term derived from "tourist" and "Klingon" used to denote a rude and irresponsible tourist.

TERRASPHERE: From the Latin *terra*, meaning earth, and *sphere*, meaning ball; i.e., a "dirtball." Useful when discussing the patient's condition with someone else while in front of the patient.

THORACOTOMY: A procedure in which the chest is cut open.

THREE HOTS AND A COT: Three meals and a bed—what homeless patients seek when they show up in the ER with a bogus complaint like, "Every time the train goes by, my feet get numb."

TOON: A loony-toon; a crazy; a mental health patient.

TRAIN WRECK: A patient with severe, complicated multisystem disease or injury.

TREAT 'EM AND STREET 'EM: Rapid turnaround time in the ER.

TRIAGE: To sort out according to severity of illness or injury, so that the more critically ill or injured patients are treated first. This runs contrary to our social custom of first come, first served, and can create resentment in the waiting room.

TROLL: A patient found under a bridge, smelling of alcohol, without a history or name.

TROLL THE LABS: To order a broad set of labs in an attempt to fish for a diagnosis in a GOMER who looks SICK but can't communicate. *See also* GOMERGRAM.

TROLLS NEVER DIE: A corollary of Murphy's Law that suggests that terrible people cannot succeed in destroying themselves however hard they try. Evidenced by the inevitable survival of the drunk driver who wipes out an entire family on their way home from Sunday morning services. It is the inverse of nice people getting cancer.

TUBED: Intubated.

VFIB: Ventricular fibrillation—a life-threatening state in which the heart quivers instead of beats. The cure is to DEFIBRILLATE or SHOCK the patient.

VTACH: Ventricular tachycardia. A rapid heart rate originating abnormally from the ventricle. Often a sign of impending VFIB or CARDIAC ARREST.

WNL: Within normal limits. Often written as a summary for some part of the physical exam, but often sarcastically interpreted as We Never Looked.

*Special thanks to those who contributed to this section: Milton H. Anderson, Eve Boyd, Keith N. Byler, Bill Davis, John Dente, Edward Dickinson, Gary M. Flashner, Corky Gordon, Donald Graham, Mike Greenberg, Charles Hagen, Hugh F. Hill, Philip Levin, Thomas J. Motycka, Scott Oslund, Gregory D. Post, Campion E. Quinn, Sylvia Sydow.*

# ACKNOWLEDGMENTS

My thanks to Anita Jones. She is my editor, consultant, writer, rewriter, and friend.

Thanks also to Frances Hall and Dartmouth Medical School. My father, the dusty professor, and his friend Nano kept me on track. Joe Bell and Sherry Angel put lots of red pencil to the stories. Readers and advisers included Steven Smith, Howard and Françoise Appel, Eve Boyd, Carol Castro, Phyllis Contini, Spencer Downing, Corky Gordon, Craig McIntyre, Barney Shapiro, Carolyn Sindell, Joe Veit, Jon Wild, and the Great Hansens: Raymond, Greg, and Theresa. Michael Eliasberg kept the lawyers at bay. Susan Sherba took care of all the paperwork. Jane Sindell and Matthew Snyder opened the door, and Andrew Blauner, Kim Witherspoon, and Craig Nelson liked the book and made me feel welcome. Special thanks to Theresa for being my companion and to Griffin for being my son.

And thank you to the hundreds of other writers who took the time to send me their stories from the Pit. It was my pleasure to read them and my regret to have been unable to use more of them.

# ABOUT THE AUTHOR

MARK W. BROWN grew up in Montana. He graduated from Harvard Law School in 1970 and practiced law in Los Angeles for nine years. In 1982, he graduated from Dartmouth Medical School, and he has practiced emergency medicine ever since.